Divine Encounters

By Brian R. Weeks

Divine Encounters

Brian R. Weeks

Copyright 2017© by Brian R. Weeks

ISBN: 978-1-61529-189-2

Vision Publishing
P.O. Box 1680
Ramona, CA 92065
1 (760) 789-4700
www.booksbyvision.org

Recommendations

"There are few times on our journey through life that we can really find someone special, and even fewer times that we find someone who truly reflects the character and nature of Jesus, a person who not only preaches the accurate word of God, but who lives it in their everyday life. A person like this is a very rare gem. Their integrity remains in great times as well as turbulent, and they remain constantly steadfast and faithful to the Spirit of God. Pastor Brian is a carbon copy of that man.

In all my years serving the Lord I've never met a man of God so committed and focused on God and His kingdom. Pastor Brian is truly a father and mentor in the kingdom of God. His ministry is one of uniqueness and of great power with signs and demonstration of the Holy Spirit. His faithfulness for more than forty years of ministry combined with an unwavering commitment have qualified him to be one of the leading voices in the modern church today. I pray that as you read through the pages of this book that it would not be just "another book," but one that transforms your life though the power of The Living God and that deepens your relationship with the Holy Spirit."

Pastor Steve Bartolomeo
Founder and former Senior Pastor, Lord of the Harvest Ministries

"I've known Pastor Brian Weeks for a number of years, and to use a comparison, I'd say that he is like a fresh breeze. He is a voice that God is using in these days to share His love, His words, and His plans for our generation. Pastor Brian is a nowadays and very accurate prophet of the Lord, whom God uses to reach His children, but also those who are not yet saved, to bring salvation, healing, deliverance, edification, and restoration. He is God's hands, feet, and mouth for today.

His prophetic messages are based on the New Covenant with grace and have a great Kingdom impact everywhere he goes. His desire is to see the Body of Christ fully equipped and enjoying God's presence. And all this comes from his intimacy with God. I have learned many things from him, and I can say that I'm very blessed to have him as a partner, friend, and brother in Christ.

Pastor Brian is a great blessing for Romania and for our church as well in the last years. He has spoken words of life over all of us, those words revealing God's heart for us and for His Church all over the world. We appreciate so much what the Lord is doing through him for impacting the nations with the Gospel of the Kingdom.

We are tremendously blessed to have him around a few weeks each year. We love his passion for The King and His Kingdom, and we are thankful to hear Pastor Brian teaching about it and to see him manifesting God's love and power through the prophetic words. This man of God has a great wisdom, a powerful revelation, and a gentle heart as a son of the Lord."

Joseph Belea, Founder and Senior Pastor
Rebirth Church, Brasov Romania

"I remember the night I first met Brian. I was a newly ordained priest in the Episcopal Church who had responded to a call to serve as the youth director for the diocese of Albany in upstate NY. My wife and I drove down to Coxsackie to help minister at an ecumenical youth event one night, and the pastor organizing the event invited us to go out to dinner with the other ministers that would be leading that night. One of the folks at the dinner was Pastor Brian, and I had been told he had a strong prophetic gift. We got to talking during the meal and before I knew it he asked me if I knew my wife and I would be having a baby soon. Ha! Well, we hadn't told anyone this yet, but we had just found out that my wife Audrey was pregnant and that we would in fact be having a baby soon. From that moment on I was certain of two things about Pastor Brian; he had an amazing prophetic anointing from the Lord, and he had the courage to say and do what Jesus wanted said and done. And that has proven true ever since. In fact, I've never met anyone who is so gifted as Brian to accomplish what Jesus wants to get done in a Christian meeting. His ability to hear the Lord so clearly and to boldly say what he hears has led to some of the most transformative encounters with Jesus that I've ever witnessed in peoples' lives."

Father Tyler Slade
Former Youth Director of the Episcopal Diocese of Albany, New York

"This book is a must-read for every Christian, especially those who have a call to leadership. I found the testimonies, insights, and lessons shared to be relevant, encouraging, and powerful. I can't wait to purchase it and use it as a part of the leadership development training in my church.

I was glued to reading the book, as I related so much of what Pastor Brian wrote to my own life. Many of the circumstances God allows--those that play a key role as He fashions us into His vessel-can be challenging and at times confusing...BUT GOD uses everything for our good if we faint not and trust Him through it all.

It never ceases to amaze me how the Lord takes such care and time to fashion us and prepare us to carry His word and presence into the lives of others. I am grateful to the Lord for the gift Brian is to the world! I am one who has been personally impacted by the ministry of the prophetic anointing on his life, and my church has been ministered to with accurate, precise, powerful words from the Lord.

Thank you, Pastor Brian, for yielding to the Holy Spirit, staying on the potter's wheel, walking through the valleys and allowing the fire to refine you. I am blessed because of your life and obedience to the call of God. Thank you for writing this book so others, just like me, will be encouraged and strengthened along their journey!"

Marlene J. Yeo
Lead Pastor - Community Christian Fellowship
Director - Somebody Cares New England
Director - He Cares For Me

Acknowledgements

You don't write a book without people who are a huge part of your life supporting and encouraging you. Since this book is an eyewitness account of what I have seen the Holy Spirit do, I have to first thank Him for allowing me to see first-hand the things He did and also for using me at times in His ministry.

Thank you to my wife Donna of 45 years for always standing by my side no matter what God did or allowed to come into our lives. To my son Josh and daughter Crystal for their continued love and support even when the church at times was not fair or loving towards us.

Thanks to close friends who <u>do</u> stick closer than brothers. Thank you to the countless people who have allowed me to be a part of their lives. It has been an honor.

Thanks also to Anne Kaminski who has spent countless hours editing this book and my first book <u>Musings</u>. Thank you for doing more than editing. Your input and suggestions have been phenomenal – Thanks, Anne.

Finally, Father, thank you for reaching through eternity and adopting me as your son.

Contents

The Early Years

God Speaks to Me

As I look back, the first time I can say God spoke to me was in the fifth grade. One very early morning around 1:30 I was woken from a dead sleep and heard a voice say to me, "Your father is coming home drunk, and he's going to hit your mother."

Problems in our house and parental arguments were nothing new, and as a child I had a big part in intervening. While the Lord would thankfully fully restore my parents' marriage years later, as a child when my parents fought, most times I would be able to step in and defuse the argument, even as young as in the fourth or fifth grade. As I reflect now on how this was possible, I understand that Isaiah 11:2 speaks of "a spirit of wisdom and understanding and a spirit of counsel." The Scriptures also tell us that the gifts and calling we receive are "irrevocable" or "without repentance." (Romans 11:29)

Indeed, when you and I were constructed in our mother's wombs God knew exactly what He wanted us to be, and He placed within each of us unique and incredible gifts. I now understand that my capacity for wisdom and counsel then and even in the present has more to do with the gifts that God placed in me and not in my own ability.

As for the first time God spoke to me, it was 10 or 15 minutes later that I looked out the window and saw my father arrive in our driveway. Soon after the fighting began, and I went downstairs to defuse the argument. Unfortunately, this time I was unsuccessful, and due to the surrounding circumstances, my mother ended up having a nervous breakdown.

The second time God spoke to me was a number of months later. I was now in the sixth grade, and we had moved from Foxboro to Attleboro, Massachusetts. My parents had decided to go out to dinner to celebrate my mom's homecoming from the hospital.

Somewhere in the middle of the night I remember being awoken again. This time I had a very clear vision in my mind that when my parents came home, the right side of my father's Mercury station wagon would be smashed in and there would be two flat tires on the right side. Sure enough, somewhere around 1:30 a.m. they drove in the driveway with two flat tires and the car smashed on the right-hand side.

All through high school friends with difficult situations in their personal lives would come to me for advice. The counsel I provided them was well beyond my age. In fact, I would have words of knowledge where I knew things about people and their circumstances without anyone providing me background or input. Sadly, when it came to my own problems however, even though I knew what to do, I rarely did it.

Again, it was clear that God had placed within me certain gifts of the Spirit which included words of wisdom, words of knowledge, and the spirit of counsel. When I went to college those gifts went with me.

College

I had worked full-time since I was 12 years old, and I didn't really want to go to college, but it was either that or the Vietnam War. By the grace of God, I got a football scholarship and off to college I went. While there I had everything that a young person would want. Because I played first-string varsity football my freshman year, I was very popular. Despite this, I spent a lot of time trying to anesthetize the pain in my heart, rather than making the most of the opportunity to get a good education.

During my third year there I was really a mess. It was sometime in the early spring that a highly hallucinogenic LSD came to campus. Probably two or three weeks prior I felt so empty inside that I sought answers at the chapel, knowing that I desperately needed help. I was attending a Baptist college in Nova Scotia yet had never, ever heard anyone there mention Jesus. In fact, I never heard them talk about religion at all.

So there I was sitting in the chapel early one morning, and I began to read the book of Revelation. I read about hell and the Lake of Fire and became very angry. I was thinking, "What kind of God would send people to hell?" I didn't realize at the time that while God offers salvation as a free gift, man rejects it and chooses eternal damnation. I become so angry that I stood up and swore at God with every profane word imaginable. I even made certain gestures with my hands and fingers expressing my anger towards this God I'd just read about.

I share this so you can better understand what happened next. I was sitting in my dorm room and had the opportunity to take LSD, so I did. Within an hour or so I was sitting down by the school administration building. I looked up in the sky and saw this dragon, a Seraphim also known as Satan, and he was laughing at me. I knew it was a Satan, because I had just read about his form in the book of Revelation.

I wasn't afraid, but it was very clear that Satan was mocking me. At this point I decided to go back to my dorm room. I jumped into bed and after 15 hours of starting the drug, I became increasingly high from its effects. I was lying there when someone knocked on my door. The person told me that what I was experiencing would last for 72 hours. He left, and I immediately got on my knees and began to pray. I don't know if you could call it prayer; it was more like a "Hey you" outburst -- "I don't know if you exist and frankly I don't care, but if you get me out of this mess within 24 hours I promise to check to see whether you're real or not."

Yes, I gave God a timeframe – 24 hours. Literally at the twenty-fourth hour to the very minute that I had specified, I was totally free from the effects of the drug without any of the typical residual after-effects. And what came of the promise that I had made to seek God if He came through? I forgot about it, or in actuality, I put it out of my mind. It was somewhere in the first seven or 10 days after the promise, however, that I was in my dorm room and a voice began to say to me, "You promised." Day after day for a few weeks I heard, "You promised, you promised."

There was young man on campus whom I had harassed for three years, and he was deathly afraid of me. Knowing that he was receiving a religious magazine, I went to see if I could borrow a copy. I knocked on his door, he opened it, and like Casper the Friendly Ghost, turned white as a sheet. I asked him for the magazine, and after he gave it to me, I went back to my room. You never know what effect you're having on someone's life just by the way you're living. He and I never spoke about faith or religion, but in that moment of seeking, I knew where to go.

Reading the magazine filled me with such peace and joy, and a few days later I heard a voice say to me, "You need to leave college now." This really didn't make any sense, as I was only five weeks from finals. My friends tried to talk me out of leaving, yet I was compelled. It was like I had no choice; I had to leave.

I arrived at the airport to fly home to see if God was real, and a freak blizzard hit. Everyone tried to convince me that I wasn't supposed to leave school but instead come back and finish. I said no but due to the snowstorm had to spend the night in the airport. The next morning, I boarded the plane, and it took off as scheduled. As I was looking out over the wing of the airplane, my right arm went up in the air all by itself. I literally had no control over it. As strange as that was, I actually began to wave like somebody on a parade float. I was waving and waving thinking, "What in the world am I doing," and yet I couldn't stop. Almost simultaneously the thought came into my mind, "You're waving goodbye to your old life."

I arrived at Logan Airport, and there was another freak blizzard, and again I ended up spending the night there. Once more I was challenged that I had made a big mistake.

My Hunger to Know Him

I arrived home, and by then God had done some amazing work healing my parents' marriage. They allowed me to stay in the garage that had been converted into a finished room. It had a bed, toilet, tile floor, and paneling. I asked for a Bible that had no cross references and no commentary. I didn't want to know anybody's opinion about who and what God was. I believed that if God was real He would reveal Himself to me, and I didn't need anybody's notes to help me prove that.

I was led to fast one, and then two days per week. I didn't have anyone tell me I should or even suggest it; I just had this desire to fast. Even when I was working construction I would alternate fasting one day the first week and two days the next. I had looked up the definition, and I understood that fasting meant to cover one's mouth.

For the first two months after coming home from college I did nothing but work, study, and pray. It was during this time that I was reading the book of Matthew, and it said that God would forgive me all my sins. I knelt on the tile floor and said, "It says here that you'll forgive me of my sins, and I'm in serious need of your forgiveness. I'm 19 years old, and I've lived the life of someone who's 40 and have made a mess of it. I've been in charge of my own life." I went on to say that He couldn't do any worse with my life than I'd done, so I wanted to give it to Him. So, there in the garage on the tile floor, I gave my life to Jesus.

My parents were meanwhile attending the Worldwide Church of God, which was considered a cult, something I didn't know at the time. Dictionary.com defines a cult as a "religion or sect considered to be false, unorthodox, or extremist with members often living outside of conventional society under the direction of a charismatic leader." Some level of mind control is often what allows the false system to exist in the first place and also for it to be sustained.

Before I started attending I did an analysis of churches. I looked at Catholic doctrine and saw some teachings with which I couldn't agree. I had attended Congregational churches before the age of 13, and they too missed the mark. I had attended a Baptist college and met there someone who wanted to be a Methodist minister yet whose life in no way reflected Christ. After what I'd personally experienced, I wanted to attend a church which literally lived and breathed what the Bible said.

So, after reading one article written by them, I began to attend the Worldwide Church of God with my parents. At the time, I didn't feel led to read their literature further or even to review their doctrines; I just wanted to read the Bible.

I remember the first day I walked into the church I saw a very attractive young lady across the sanctuary. I heard a voice say to me, "You're looking at your wife." Later I learned that the young woman I saw was the same young girl who had visited my family and their restaurant/hotel business just as I was leaving for college. At the time, she was entering high school, and there had been no connection at all. But there I was three years later seeing my future wife. At the time of this book's writing, Donna and I have been married 45 years.

My first year in the church all I did was pray, study, work, and clean the church bathrooms. The second year I was asked to take over a youth group of 14 teens. One year later, we had 105. At the time, I thought it was because I was cool and clever, but I know now that nothing could have been further from the truth. I was simply operating in the favor of God and with the gifts He had given me. In fact, years later God spoke to me and said, "You can't be clever and anointed at the same time."

It was also during the second year that I started to group date. For me it was just companionship. I didn't actually date Donna until my third year in the church, because before that point she hadn't fully committed herself to Christ, and I didn't want her to make that decision for my sake; I wanted her to do it for herself. In June she made the commitment, and I immediately asked her out. By November I spent three and a half days fasting, asking God if I should marry her.

At the end of the three and a half days God hadn't answered me. I finally prayed and told him that if at the end of seven days He hadn't told me <u>not</u> to, that I would ask her. Two weeks later I did just that, and at that moment I kissed her for the first time. Thereafter though, we never sat around kissing. In fact, whenever we hugged I would put a pillow between us, because I had done it so wrong in the past I didn't want to mess it up again.

We were married at the end of January 1972, and our son was born in December of that same year.

Miracle Birth and Surrender

Donna went into labor on Christmas Eve and was in labor 36 hours, over 10 of them hard labor. We had decided on home birth and had found a midwife in her late sixties who'd delivered 686 children without a fatality. After 10 hours of Donna pushing, she started to bleed. At that moment, I decided to go into the bathroom to pray, and on the way there overheard the midwife say, "I think the baby is dead."

I knelt down on the floor, grabbing the old sweaty porcelain toilet and praying this way: "I love you, I love my wife, and I love my son." (I actually didn't know for sure it was going to be a boy.) I told God that if my son died it would not change anything; I would continue to love and serve him. If my wife died it wouldn't change anything; I would love and serve Him, and if both died, the same would be true. I never thought about calling for an ambulance.

I went back into the bedroom, and within a minute our son was born. While he didn't breathe right away, suddenly he started to breathe and was then fine. The moment required a very deep place of surrender, which I am now thankful for, because that's been my life's journey all along - a life of yielding and submission.

Seven years later and after two miscarriages, Donna and I had our daughter. It was our deep faith and love for God and His love for us that got us through losing those two children.

Demons are Real

I started preaching when I was 22 years old, and since I had never read or studied the church's doctrine and had only read the Bible, I began to teach New Testament theology. I used to wonder how I ended up in a religious cult. The answer is simple and is found in Psalm 37:23 (AMP): "The steps of a [good and righteous] man are directed and established by the Lord; And He delights in his way [and blesses his path]." It was clear to me that I had been such a lawless person that I needed the law which the Worldwide Church of God taught. If I had been born again into grace I don't know if I would still be walking with God today.

The cult served as my training ground in so many different ways. I remember one afternoon I wanted to drop off my weekly youth report to the pastor, so I called him to tell him I'd leave it at his house. He told me not to come because he was in the middle of something. About a half hour later though, he called and had changed his mind, so I got in my car and drove to his home in Rhode Island.

When I walked into the house there was a young lady in her early 20s, about five feet two, weighing approximately a hundred and fifteen pounds. She was levitating in midair about four feet off the ground. The pastor and the elder who was with him pushed her down to the ground, yet as soon as they let go she came back up in the air again and remained in midair all by herself. At this point it became obvious that they'd asked me to come over to help them deal with this problem.

The Worldwide Church of God believed that a person could not be demonized and saved at the same time. I knew the girl and that she had committed her life to Christ. Even though the church had wrong theology, she had genuinely made that commitment. The church also didn't believe the scripture from John 10:16 about Jesus saying that His sheep hear His voice. How sad it is that most churches don't teach that Jesus meant what he said, that because we are in a relationship we can actually hear Him speak to us.

The three of us began to pray. When we started, the scripture from Luke 8:30 came to mind where Jesus asks the demon his name. So, I followed suit. A man's voice proceeded to come out of this young girl, and the demon gave us his name. At that point in time I spoke to the demon by his name and told him he had to leave. The girl became limp, so we thought that we had been successful in casting the demon out. We then let go of her, and once again she levitated about four feet in the air.

Again, I asked the demon what his name was, and he replied that the first demon had left and that he was now in charge. We repeated this pattern for about an hour and 15 minutes with no real change except that different voices would come out of the girl as she continued to levitate in mid-air. Even though I was the youngest of everyone in the room I was the one to suggest, "Why don't we stop trying to cast out demons and just pray."

During our prayer, the Lord spoke to me that the first demon never left. Even though this church doesn't believe a person can hear God, I turned to the pastor and elder and told them what God had told me, that the first demon we told to leave never did and that the demon was lying to us. The demon then started laughing at us in such a way that the hair could have stood up on our arms and legs. He said to us, "You don't know what you're doing," and unfortunately the demon was right. Even though we were using the name of Jesus, we didn't believe there was power in His name.

In Acts 3:16 it points out that you must have faith in the name of Jesus. What does that mean? We were using Jesus' name but not really having faith in its power and authority. We might as well have said, "Abracadabra." We held the girl down, and then the pastor decided to call his overseeing pastor to ask him what we should do. He returned and told us that he had been instructed to stop what we were doing and take the girl home. After about 20 minutes the girl became normal and didn't remember what had just happened. They decided that I should take her home, and so I did.

Amazingly the story about this demon does not end there. It was about 12 years later that a different woman called me, said she was having trouble, and asked if she could come for prayer. At that point, I was the associate pastor in a church in Rehoboth, Massachusetts called Christian Life Fellowship. The woman came over, we sat at my kitchen table, and I suggested that we pray.

As I began I heard her tapping on the table, and she was spitting saliva out of her mouth. At that very moment, I knew that the demon I had failed to deal with 12 years earlier was the same demon that I was facing now. I said to the demon, "Twelve years ago I didn't know how to deal with you, but today I know." I said that I was going to set this woman free and that the demon would have to leave her. The demon which was again using a man's voice, said to me that it would leave but would find my family and kill them.

I told the demon that that wasn't possible because my family was under the blood of Jesus. I quoted the scripture in Exodus 12 which speaks about how when the destroyer saw the blood on the door posts of the children of Israel in Egypt it had to pass over, and no harm would come to those under the blood. I told the demon that I had better blood than the blood that covered the doorpost in the book of Exodus. The blood that covered my family was better blood than that of sheep and goats, because they had the blood of Jesus covering them. Since the blood of Jesus covered my family, when the demon saw them it had to pass over and not harm them. I told the demon it had to leave in the name of Jesus, and immediately by the grace and love of God this woman was set free.

As the book continues I will go into further detail of the time period between 1980 and 1992 when it was a fairly common for me to deal with people who were demonized.

God indeed used the Worldwide Church of God to teach me many things and to deal with a number of issues in my life. To this day God is still dealing with issues in my life. In fact, for all of us this life is a continual journey of being transformed into the likeness of Jesus.

God's Shaping

I was about 24 years old when the church determined to ordain me as a minister.

The day came when we had a combined ordination service with another church, the ordination of pastors a big event. I sat there very excited as we completed the first service. The plan was to have lunch and then come back and have the second service during which I would be among the three ordained.

Just before lunch, however, the pastor called me to come see him on the stage. He told me that the headquarters church had decided that based on the size of the congregation, they didn't want to ordain three men in one day and that he had decided not to ordain me. He explained that the reason he'd made that decision was that I was respected, people followed my leadership, and that I "didn't need the title."

I can't begin to tell you the struggle I had sitting through the second service where the two other men were ordained. Many years later though, I truly understand that it was the grace of God that I wasn't ordained that day. You see, God had a bigger picture in mind which involved chipping away my immense pride. Within a few weeks I truly understood that I didn't need a title to serve God or to be a leader. I simply needed to be a servant.

That one event deeply shaped my entire approach to ministry which became that of simply being a servant and not looking for a name or prestige. I recalled the scripture where Jesus said he made Himself of no reputation (Philippians 2:7). So, if Jesus made Himself of no reputation, why should I be concerned about mine? I would learn this lesson over and over and over again, and even to this day I'm still learning this very simple lesson. As you have already discovered, God works in us even in areas that we don't want Him to, and it's all because He loves us and is molding and transforming us into the image of His son Jesus.

Jumping ahead to 1976, I was working for a demolition construction company in Boston, Massachusetts and also serving in ministry 20 hours a week. One Monday morning on my construction job I was asked to cut a hole in a solid wall in preparation for installing a window. The building was constructed in the early 1800s, and at the time they didn't use cement for the joints; they used limestone. There was shoring to my left to hold up the 6x12 timber floor joists, and to the right of me was a newly-cut hole in the floor for a trash shoot.

As I was cutting the hole in the wall for a window, a voice spoke to me saying, "Look up." As I looked up I saw the entire wall section heading towards me. I only had one way to go and turned around and ran as quickly as I could. I was only two steps out before I was buried in brick. Later they calculated that the weight of the brick was over 2,000 pounds, and this did not include the velocity of how far it fell. Those who saw it happen thought I was dead, and I should have been. Just two days after, a similar accident happened in Seekonk, and three men died when a block wall fell on them.

This incident resulted in my being out of work for three and half years, and I suffered with a great deal of pain for five. Although I was taking large amounts of medication to try to bring some relief to the pain, the meds were never effective. It was during this same time that the pastor of the church I was serving in came and told me that I needed to stop preaching New Testament theology. I asked him if he believed that what I was preaching was true, and he responded that he did. I asked him, "Then why don't you preach it?" and he said, "Because I would be fired." I responded and said, "So you're worried about a paycheck?" and he answered in the affirmative.

He went on to say that if I continued to preach the same stuff that he would have to kick me out. I said I would do him a favor and spare him the trouble by leaving first. It was only a couple weeks after my departure when he stood up in the pulpit and told the congregation not to have anything to do with me because I was preaching heresy (Romans 16:17). All at once my wife and I lost all of our friends and our relationships. For the next three and a half years we were isolated and except for a brief time, had no fellowship with other Christians, even though I had co-planted the congregation.

It was during this time period that we had our gas and electricity shut off more than once and eventually ended up several months behind in our mortgage. We decided that we were going to sell the house rather than having it foreclosed on and called Donna's father to ask him for the name of a realtor. He said they would get back to us, but before he did, Donna's grandmother called and asked why we were selling the house. We told her that it was because we were falling behind in the mortgage and other bills, to which she replied that she would take care of them. She did. Thankfully she stepped in, because at the same time the engine of our car blew up, and we were unable to drive it.

Meanwhile I was living on the floor for three and a half years because it was too painful to sleep in a bed. I was also in and out of hospitals. It was during the gas embargo in the late 70s that I ended up in a pain clinic for nine weeks where they taught me how to walk again without crutches and detoxed me off all medication. I succeeded in learning to walk assist-free and also how to live with pain, but when the stress of normal life returned, so did the need for medication.

Believing God for Healing

I want you to think for a moment about how much pain I was in. I had nerve damage, arthritis, and a ruptured disc in my back. I was taking 120 Percodan and 60 valium a week plus a barbiturate to allow me to sleep for at most, four hours a night. I would lie on the floor and cry for hours. In order for me to help with dinner I would have to take 2.5 Percodan and even then, I was still in agony. When I would go to the bathroom and sit, within 30 seconds I wouldn't feel anything below my waist. I couldn't put my full weight on the floor, so I used crutches. Whenever I had to go into the car I would lie in the back seat crying, asking Donna to avoid bumps and pot holes. I was never pain-free. During my nine-weeks in the pain clinic, they documented that I couldn't sit or stand for more than five minutes at a time,

The day of the accident the church elder came and prayed for me. I was put on every prayer line you can imagine. I mean, you name the ministry prayer line, and I was on it. Each passing minute was beyond agonizing. Here I am a man of God believing for healing, and nothing is happening. I also had my share of Job's friends with their "opinions and conclusions." For five years I believed God would heal me, and I never once gave up on His ability to do it. I never got angry at Him. I realize now that the faith that I had was supernatural. It wasn't *my* faith per se, but God holding onto me and assuring me that the day would come when I would be healed.

I had the incredible love and support of Donna as well. What a rock she was! She did everything during a time when there was a lot of emotional pain in addition to the physical. I had always dreamed of having a son and sharing special memories, for example. So, one of the most painful moments I experienced was when Josh asked me to throw him a baseball. I couldn't, so someone else had to step in. Also painful was when I watched someone else teach him to ride a bike. Josh was a great help to Donna, but he grew up faster than he should have.

During all this God was using the time to kill the pharisee in me. I was full of self-righteousness and pride prior to the accident and couldn't understand how a Christian could make a bad decision. Well, I learned how under the right pressure and circumstances great Christians make bad choices. In the end, I realized that as I

Peter 1:5 says, I was "kept by the power of God." I assure you Our Father does an awesome job of "keeping us."

By God's grace I was believing He would heal me. Finally, in December of 1980 I had back surgery. Within 10 days I was no longer taking any medication. I was totally pain-free. The nerve damage and arthritis were totally gone.

If you're waiting for a miracle, you can take it from me first-hand… keep on believing.

God Gives Us a House and Then He Keeps It

I probably should write about the miracle of how we ended up with a house in the first place. Right after Donna and I got married I was laid off from the construction job I had and started a window cleaning business that I hated but at which I made good money. During the time, I was out of work for a while, I was collecting an unemployment check of $74.00 a week. The church taught that each year 10 percent of our gross was to be given for the Levities and 10 percent of our gross to attend the Holy Days spoken of in Deuteronomy 16:16-17: "Three times a year all your males shall appear before the Lord your God in the place which He chooses: at the Feast of Unleavened Bread, at the Feast of Weeks, and at the Feast of Tabernacles; and they shall not appear before the Lord empty-handed. Every man shall give as he is able, according to the blessing of the Lord your God which He has given you."

Then Deuteronomy 14:28-29 tells that every three years you were to give another 10 percent for widows, orphans, and strangers. This was my third tithe year. So, if you do the math, it is three times $7.50, or $22.50, which amounted to $51.50 we had after tithing. We gave a $5.00 offering as well, which meant we were left with a total income of $47.50 a week.

While working construction I made $350 a week, and after taxes my take-home pay was $225. If you multiply $35 times three tithes, the total is $105. Add our offering of five dollars, and our giving totaled $110, which left $115 a week for our bills. We couldn't afford to pay our car payment, our rent, or our MasterCard balance. Our landlord saw me and asked me why I couldn't pay him. Sadly, instead of telling him about Jesus, I told him about tithing. He said that while he respected me for my convictions, he was still going to evict us. MasterCard had already visited Donna, so we tore up our credit card; then Chrysler arrived at our home to repossess our car. We had $10 in the bank. There seemed to be only one option--move into my parents' home

At the same time Donna's father asked us to come visit him because he wanted us to buy the home Donna grew up in so he that could purchase a new one. How could we tell him no? We drove down to Somerset from North Attleboro, and like a realtor he showed us the home, assuring us that it was worth $31,500 but that he would sell it to us for $26,500. I thanked him but said we couldn't afford it and also had no money for a down payment.

We went home, and about a week later Donna's grandmother asked us to come down to Somerset to talk about purchasing the house. When we started talking I told her that the price her father offered us was tremendous, but I didn't have a down payment. She got up, walked into her bedroom, picked up the bed mattress, opened her hope chest, and then searched in her dresser. When she came out she put $8,000 on the coffee table and asked, "Will this help?" I was thinking that even with this money for a down payment, no bank would give us a loan. We thanked her, took the money, and within a few days went and applied for a mortgage. I never thought they would approve us.

I put $7,000 down and kept $1,000 for closing costs. Within three days the bank called us and said we had been approved for the mortgage. Within thirty days we closed on the home with closing costs at $400. That left us with $600, so we went out to dinner and paid off some bills. Our one bedroom furnished apartment cost us $164 a month. Our mortgage, insurance, and taxes were $165 a month, and her father left all but the living room furniture. We had three bedrooms of furniture, a washer, dryer, and all the appliances. Can you say miracle?

Things were going fine until 1976 when a brick wall fell on me. I was out of work for months but needed to return to pay our bills. I was able to work for a few years though was in agony 24 hours a day. I finally stopped working and was out for three and a half years. You can imagine the debt we incurred, because workers' compensation was only one-third of my salary. During this time, the gas was shut off twice as well as the electricity. We were broke, and I was still in agony.

By this time, it was 1980, and by the grace of God the doctor I had seen to apply for Social Security Disability advised me to go back to see my neurologist to tell him that in his opinion, I had a serious back problem. In the hospital, I ended up sharing a room with a young man who was attending a small home cell group that was only four houses from mine. One particular evening 20 or so people showed up in our hospital room and all began praying in the spirit, in tongues. This was the first time that I'd prayed in tongues with a group of people.

It was during the time when I was out of work and living on the floor that one day I read the scriptures in Acts two where it speaks about being baptized in the Holy Spirit and speaking with other tongues (Acts 2). I told the Lord that if that was real, I wanted it. He said to me, "Go ahead and start speaking, but I don't want you using English or Spanish," Spanish being a language I'd learned in college and English of course, my native tongue.

I started speaking using only vowels and consonants, and I was like a baby trying to speak without the ability to articulate words. I had two voices in my head: one saying it was only me and the other saying that it was God helping me to speak another language. It was a struggle between the expression of God's heart and the devil's attempt at stopping me. I remembered that children in their cribs don't speak fluently at first either.

It was a number of years later that Donna, who wanted nothing to do with speaking in tongues, had her own divine encounter. We were faced with a life-altering decision. We were standing in our front room and began to pray. Honestly, we really didn't know how to pray. All of a sudden there was Donna speaking fluently in another language, her experience so different from mine. There is no formula to speaking in tongues—all I know is if you want to, you will. I also know that if you need an answer, God will give you one.

After Surgery God Provides

It was sometime in the spring after surgery that I had applied the second time for Social Security Disability. When I had applied previously the attorney failed to file an appeal after I was denied. Donna and I were now eight months behind in our mortgage and received a foreclosure notice from the bank. We were over $8,000 in debt and needed a car. We hired a new attorney, and I appeared before a judge for him to determine whether or not I was eligible to receive disability. The judge kept shaking his head as he reviewed the over one-foot-high pile of medical records.

The hearing ended, and we waited for a decision. It was the middle of June when we received a letter in the mail. Before we opened it Donna and I sat and prayed on a love seat whose springs were very nearly poking through. Our prayer was "Father, thank you for your decision. Whether we win or lose we want to thank you. Everything is in your hands." We opened the letter, and there was a check for $25,000. We paid off all our debt, bought a used car (story forthcoming), and put the rest away to supplement our income (another story).

God Provides a Car

We needed a vehicle, so off we went to the car auction. I was shocked at the prices, and there was nothing there that drew my attention besides the cost of used cars. I went back the following week with our car mechanic. I was looking around and spotted a

1980 Oldsmobile Cutlass which I loved. It came into the auction, but my mechanic wasn't around. The car didn't end up being sold, however, because the bid of $5,300 was turned down. After my mechanic showed up I told him the story, and he told me to go and look again.

As I looked around, there was the Cutlass. They had put a new number on it so that they could bring it back into the auction later that day. I went over to the car and laid my hands on it saying, "Lord, I do not want to pay any more than $5,500 for this car." He responded by saying, "I know how much you can afford." The car came into the auction, and the price went to $5,200. The auctioneer was looking for another bid, and I told the mechanic to go ahead. He replied that the last bid was mine, and it would be foolish to bid again.

They closed the bidding, yet I was thinking that because they turned down more money in the morning, I had no chance of getting the car. The auctioneer turned to the car dealer and asked him what he wanted to do. The dealer said, "Let the guy have the car." Another miracle.

God Provides a Job and Promotions

It was July fourth. I was on a 21-day fast when we went to Donna's parents for a holiday picnic. Donna's step brother was there, and he worked at ADP, a national payroll company whose Rhode Island office was in East Providence. I hadn't worked in three and a half years and wasn't sure if my body could take working again. Kiddingly, I asked him if there was any work available in his company. He responded yes, that there was a job open on third shift.

That week I applied for the job. The director of operations conducted the interview, as the HR person was on leave. He took one look at my application and said I was over-qualified due to my college coursework. He asked me my eventual job goal within their company, and I told him that I wanted his job! He laughed, and the interview ended. I returned home and went to my bedroom to pray. I was praying and wondering if I should take the job if they offered it to me. Remember that I had just had back surgery and hadn't worked in three years. At that very moment, the phone rang and sure enough, the job was mine!

I took the job making $4.25 an hour. (It occurred to me that I'd made more money at 13 when I helped to support our family when my father was in New Hampshire fixing up a hotel and restaurant he'd purchased.) Anyway, after a three-month probation period, they offered me a quarter per hour raise, and I got to keep my job.

This was nuts - four dollars and twenty-five cents an hour - now you can see why God provided the Social Security check! I told my brother-in-law that while I was thankful for them taking a risk on me, I couldn't live on that amount of pay. A few days later I was called into the HR office, and they offered me a newly-created position of group leader of my department with a significant raise in pay. This did not go over well with the three other people in the department! One man had been there nine years, another five, and the other approximately three. The man who had worked there nine years didn't talk to me for two weeks.

A year went by, and they called me into the HR office. They offered me a promotion to another job which due to my group leader position, resulted in a large cut in pay. I asked if I could speak to the general manager. They said, "Sure, go to Bart's office." So off to his office I went.

When I arrived, he stood to greet me and then closed the door. I told him my reason for being there, and he responded by asking me how I'd like to become the company's credit manager. I told him that I had no experience in finances, which he said was no problem. I then pointed out that they already had a credit manager, to which he responded that they were planning to let her go. "What about posting the job," I asked, to which he said there would be no problem as they'd design the qualifications based on my resume. I asked if there would be an increase in salary, and he said there would be. I told him I needed to go home and pray about it, and so I did.

Within a couple hours I got a call from HR, and they told me that I was going to get about a three dollar per hour raise and that my role would be to collect money from delinquent accounts. I wasn't very good at confrontation, but God uses circumstances to teach us things we need to learn. Apparently, what I needed to learn was accounting and how to confront people. I took the job.

The Holy Spirit Directs Me at Work

My new job involved calling our clients on the phone to ask for the money they owed our company. While talking with them, I would often get words of wisdom and words of knowledge and also ended up praying with them over situations in their lives. Over the next year, I became the number one credit manager in all the 55 ADP offices in America and Canada.

Month after month, I was the number one credit manager, and as a reward they would send Donna and I out to dinner on the company, which was our favorite thing to do. They awarded me the Credit Manager of the Year, and staff from the corporate office came down to give me the award, present me with a bonus, and take me out to dinner. They also arrived with a job offer.

Because the balance on my accounts was so low, they wanted me to travel to the various branches and teach and train them regarding how I collected money. The vice president of corporate asked me if I could show him how I did it. I said I'd be glad to. We went over to my cubicle, and I sat down and slid the outstanding accounts printout in front of me. They called it an aging because the printout contained accounts that were over 30, 60, or 90 days late. I took my two hands and laid them on the printout. Then I looked at him and said, "I pray the money in."

The vice president of corporate laughed. He turned to the general manager and said, "He's kidding, isn't he?" The general manager replied that indeed I was not. It was known throughout the entire company that I would call people on the phone and pray with them and prophecy to them. In this and in every situation, I was compelled to be who I was. The vice president of corporate took me to dinner and never made the offer to me again.

Bart approached me a few months later and said he wanted to make me the company controller. He added that his desire was to send me back to college to get a degree in finance. He said it would take a year or year and a half, and they wanted me to return to school and get the degree. "We'll pay you your full salary and you don't even have to work," he said. I thanked him for the job offer, which was pretty amazing. I told him, though, that I needed to go home and pray.

The next day I came in and thanked Bart and told him that God had called me to full-time ministry. If I took the offer it would mean that he and ADP would never get back the investment they had made in me. He was shocked and said that if he didn't promote me he'd lose me. He needed to leave for vacation but said that when he returned he wanted to talk to me again.

When he got back he told me that they had created a new position between second and third shift. It was for a director of operations and came with a very large increase in salary. I accepted the position and had it for about a year and a half. It was during this time that Bart got a call from the ADP in Boston who wanted to know if I was interested in becoming their credit manager. The offer included a salary of a $100,000 a year, a new car, and gas card. They would also pay to move me from Somerset to the Waltham area.

They said I could make my own hours but wanted me to work at least 20 a week. I asked Bart what he had said to them, and he replied that he'd told them that I was going into full-time ministry and couldn't take the job. I told Bart that he was correct. A few months went by and the Hartford, Connecticut office called with a similar type of offer. Their salary was more than $100,000 a year and as with the other position, Bart told them I wouldn't take the job. Again, I told him that he was right.

It was shortly after this that the door opened for me to go into the ministry full-time. At this point I was working in both my secular and ministry jobs for 40 hours a week each.

My final day at ADP was quite memorable. I had started there as the lowest paid person in the company. Five years later, besides the employees working in sales, I was leaving them as the seventh highest paid person in the entire company! As I was walking out the door I heard the Holy Spirit say to me, "You'll never work a secular job again." That was in 1987, and it has proven true. Even though twice I've started churches with no money, I've never worked a secular job since. (An interesting note is that a few months after I left ADP, the director of operations was transferred to the ADP in Waltham. More than likely if I had stayed there I would've had his job.)

It's critical at every juncture of our lives to hold true to our vision and follow the Holy Spirit. It requires a willingness to make sacrifices and hard choices, with every decision being made through the vision for our lives. Each of us can hear and be led by the Holy Spirit, and every day matters. There's no switch to activate between the church and secular society. We are called to be sons and daughters of God 24 hours a day in whatever situation we find ourselves.

The Holy Spirit Starts a Church

If you remember, I mentioned the cell group meeting in my neighborhood? Well, it was just before Christmas 1981 when the group left food and an envelope of $300 on our door step. They, and in particular Pastor Tony Saraiva, would split wood that was sitting in our driveway, as wood was the means of heating our home. There were no strings attached; they were simply acts of love. On New Year's Eve, they were having a bible study, and I went to thank them for everything they'd done and given us. I was welcomed and loved as if they had known me for years, and I can look back and recall feeling for the very first time the tangible presence of God in a meeting.

I continued to attend, and it was near Easter when they asked me to be an elder in this small group of 25 people. I can remember going home and telling Donna this news. She was not attending and responded that they hadn't asked us but instead, just me. I said that if they'd asked me, they'd asked us. She agreed, because she didn't want to stand in the way of my calling.

It was June of 1981 that God spoke to Pastor Tony (simply Tony at the time) that our cell group was to put on a tent meeting to preach Jesus. In fact, the meetings were called Tent Meetings for Jesus.

A handful of us began planning and preparing to put on a tent meeting on Route 138 in Somerset, Massachusetts. None of us wanted to preach because we weren't looking to build a church; we simply wanted to teach the gospel. We hired an Irish evangelist who came and set up a tent which held 400 people.

We were hoping that 50 or 60 people would attend each night and were amazed that instead the tent was filled with over 400, with about 300 sitting on the grass outside. We saw such incredible signs and wonders it was staggering. We saw deaf people hear, blind people see, and one man with a severely broken leg be miraculously healed. The man came for prayer and then the next day went to see his doctor. His intent in doing this was to stand up at the tent meeting and tell everyone that healing was a farce and simply untrue.

He had recently broken his leg, and at the doctor's he insisted they take an X-ray. To his and the doctor's amazement, his leg was totally healed. That night the man stood up in front of everyone holding the cast that had been cut off in one hand and x-rays of the spiral fracture in the other. Without any prompting, he began running around the exterior of the tent. It was a sight that you had to see to believe!

For seven days, we witnessed miracle after miracle. We saw couples - husbands and wives - come to the front of the altar to be prayed with, and as we prayed with them they would both simultaneously fall down under the power of God. As the Irish preacher would preach he would point to a section of chairs that had been tied together because of the fire codes. He would say, "The Spirit of God is over here," and at that moment 40 chairs with people sitting in them would all flip over backwards at the same time. We saw hundreds of people commit their lives to Christ.

As the tent came down people asked us if they could come to our church. We told them that we weren't a church per se and that besides, we had no room for more people at our cell group. We would give them a list of churches in the area, but most said, "We don't want to go to those churches. We want to come to where you are."

Within a few weeks we began feeling that God wanted us to host a Sunday night service but not to become a church. I remember our first Sunday night we were standing in a broom closet praying, so nervous we had no idea who would even show up. To our amazement 75 people came, and we continued to grow every Sunday night after that. We hadn't planned who would or wouldn't speak; we just decided that we would let God lead us. I remember how powerful it was to share the simple gospel. We ended up praying for people, and there in this rented hall people would fall under the power of God. He thus began the birth of what eventually became Christian Life Fellowship.

We soon outgrew this small rented hall whose bathrooms I cleaned after the place was used as a bar on Saturday nights. You can just imagine what that was like! Arrangements were then made for us to meet on Sunday nights in the local Methodist church. In a very short time that meeting grew to about 175 people. We began holding Saturday Sunday school in my home. Shortly after that we heard the Holy Spirit say to us, "You're playing church, and you need to become a church." So, with fear and trepidation we rented a building in Swansea called the Holy Ghost Hall. We had no idea how many of the 175 people who were attending the Sunday evening service would even come. We were staggered and amazed as we held our first meeting, and 110 people showed up. Within a very short time the Lord spoke to us to find property and build a church. From the time of our first service in 1981 until the time that God spoke to me to leave and start my own church in 1992, the church grew to about 700 people.

The Christian Life Fellowship Years and the Power of God

It would take volumes of books to express all the things that God did during the next 10 years, but here is a snapshot.

We continued to hold tent meetings and see the Holy Spirit move on thousands of lives. Thousands of people attended, and thousands of people committed their lives to Jesus. I even saw my niece and nephew from Michigan give their lives to Jesus. Later Britt became a minister and Lisa married a young man who became a pastor.

I'll share just a few things I saw and of which I was honored to be a part. It was during the third year of hosting the tent meetings that the mother and father of a 10-year-old girl came into the tent. They were driving by on their way home from the hospital. Earlier that day they had been to a local carnival when someone accidentally poked their daughter in the eye with a pretzel, resulting in a complete loss of vision to the girl's left eye. I remember when they were standing in front of me. They had never seen a miracle; they weren't Christians. One thing was clear though; they were desperate.

I asked if I could remove the bandage that covered her left eye, and they gave me permission. I then gently placed my hand on her blind eye and prayed a simple prayer. Within moments the girl began to cry and turned to hug her parents, saying, "I can see." They went to the doctor's the next day and verified that her sight was restored one hundred per cent.

There was another night when we were meeting, and I saw a man in a wheelchair roll his chair to the front for prayer. I was thinking, "I sure hope someone else prays for him." My wish was not to be, because in a few minutes I looked up and he was there in front of me. Not having a whole lot of faith, I prayed for him. After we prayed he asked me if I would help him out of his chair. What was I going to say? I helped him up, and this look came across his face that I'll never forget.

There at that moment God didn't just heal him; God did a creative miracle. The man hadn't walked in over 10 years!

On another night, a woman came for prayer, and as she was prayed for she fell under the power of God and moments later was levitating in midair. Since I had seen this before, I thought to myself, "No problem." As I prayed she fell to the ground and started screaming. Seconds later she was standing up and was totally delivered from a demon that had harassed her for years.

One of my favorite memories of so many happened one night as we were praying for an elderly woman. She stood in front of me and was telling me this very sad story. All of a sudden, I was filled with such joy that I asked her to excuse me. I took a couple of steps away from her and broke into a laughter that can't be described. Then I fell over backwards and laid there for probably 20 minutes and couldn't get up. I was trying to tell my brain to tell my legs to move, but they wouldn't cooperate. I asked a couple of ushers to stand me up. My legs still wouldn't move. The ushers held me up as I continued to pray for people. As soon as I touched their hands every person broke into spontaneous laughter. At the end of the night there were about 30 or so workers, maybe more, standing there with skeptical looks on their faces. I asked them all to join hands and then took my hands and completed the circle. Instantaneously every single person broke into laughter.

You might ask why I laughed in response to the woman's prayer. I want to emphasize that I walked away from the woman so as to not laugh in her face. There are times when we are sad and depressed, and God's antidote is called laughter. Proverbs 17:22 (AMPC) says, "A happy heart is good medicine, and a cheerful mind works healing, but a broken spirit dries up the bones." Just imagine how many people our Father healed that night through laughter. I have to believe that God in His love for this woman touched her as only He could.

During the years at Christian Life we saw such signs and wonders. We saw people healed by the hundreds. There was a period of two years that everyone I prayed for with cancer was healed. Service after service the Holy Spirit would move. To be honest we didn't know what we were doing. We hadn't copied anyone; in fact, what was happening with us was not happening in the majority of other churches anywhere. We went through the tongues movement, then prophecy, then song of the Lord, and then deliverance.

Eventually because we or I (speaking for myself), lacked the character to go along with the move of God, it stopped. I can say of myself that I was like Sampson. I had the anointing but I didn't have the character that was needed. As we look at the life of Sampson we see that he was used powerfully by God in spite of his moral failures, but in the end those failures led to his capture.

My personal character flaws included pride and self-righteousness. Instead of being humbled that God was using me, I began to indulge myself with feeling important. I forgot the source of the anointing, and it led me to an attitude of self-righteousness. I saw myself as better. God loved me so much, however, that He couldn't allow this character flaw to continue. Thus, by the time I started my first church in 1992, my prophetic anointing had dried up. When I asked the Lord where my prophetic anointing was He told me that He didn't want the church built on my prophetic gift but instead on the most important gift - His Son.

The Beginning of Prophetic Ministry

My prophetic ministry started in 1981 when a group of us were standing in a home in Fall River poised to pray for a woman who was sick. I had a very basic prophetic word revealing the reason for her sickness. As with any gift that God gives us, I needed to use it in order for it to grow and be developed. From this prophetic word in that first home I began to give general prophetic words in church and at cell groups, which are in and of themselves a great venue to exercise one's gifting.

Then the Holy Spirit gave me the courage to begin giving very specific and direct words to people in private. This progressed to giving direct words to people (especially new people) in church. The Holy Spirit would also use this prophetic gift in a very dynamic way during counseling and deliverance sessions.

The Holy Spirit in a Field

It was late in April 1981 that I was struggling with what the truth was. Every day I was at the table with my arms full of books. As I was studying there was a conflict between what I was reading in commentaries and what was in my mind.

In fact, I had conflict that existed on four fronts. One, the Holy Spirit which Jesus said would teach us was trying to reveal to me *real* truth. Two, the church I was in had severe errors when it came to many doctrines and overall biblical principles. Thirdly, many of the commentaries I was studying were written by theologians who were not believers in their heart. Intellectual in orientation, they discussed history, grammar, and definitions of Hebrew and Greek words using human reasoning, yet without the indwelling Holy Spirit. The fourth conflict was my own natural mind.

Thankfully one day God spoke to me and asked if I was tired of teaching myself. He reminded me of the scripture in John when Jesus said that the Holy Spirit would teach us. *"But the Helper, the Holy Spirit, whom the Father will send in My name, He will teach you all things."* (John 14:26 NKJV)

He went on to tell me to put all my books away and to let Him teach me. I promptly got up, put the books away, and within a short period of time went out into a field through the woods a good distance from my home. No houses were nearby. I had brought a yellow blanket to kneel on and had my Bible. I began to shout, "What is the truth?" Louder and louder I shouted it. I reached over and started pulling up grass and throwing it in the air. I was lamenting much in the same way the Jews would take dirt and throw it in the air, letting it fall on their heads. I wanted God to speak to me.

After a while God asked me the question, "What are you doing?" I told him that I was trying to get His attention so that He would speak to me. He said, "I'll tell you what you're doing. You're getting dirty hair." Discouraged I picked up everything and went home.

As I reached the door of my house, the phone was ringing. I threw everything on the floor and picked up the phone. A woman asked me if my name was Brian Weeks, and I told her it was. She said, "God wants to tell you that he is not deaf."

I haven't yelled at God since and now always let Him teach me.

The Holy Spirit in a Broom Closet

I remember one beautiful summer afternoon when a couple who had been dating for years got married. They had finally made the decision. The groom was very late in arriving, and when he got close to me it was obvious he was intoxicated, so much so that he could barely stand up. So now what? A hundred and fifty people were waiting for the wedding to start.

The Holy Spirit told me to take him and his fiancé into this large broom closet where I was to lay hands on him. I obeyed, and the three of us went in. We stood there, and I laid my hands on him, at which point he crashed to the floor. He laid there and finally began to stir. When he got up he was completely sober, and their wedding ended up being very beautiful.

The Holy Spirit Delivers People

From 1981 until 1992 God used me in deliverance in a tremendous way. I was dubbed the deliverance pastor of Southeast New England. Dozens of students would come from a nearby Christian College seeking deliverance from being demon-oppressed.

We used to host a monthly coffee house. One night a young lady came to the church for the first time. As soon as she walked into the foyer she collapsed; her eyes were rolling back in her head, she was foaming at the mouth, and uttering strange noises. Guess who they came to get? We took her into my office and within a very few minutes she was delivered and yes, ended up committing her life to Christ.

On a Sunday night during an evening service was another interesting occurrence. In the middle of worship, a woman was in the back of the church on her hands and knees howling like a dog. One word and she was free.

On a Sunday morning during worship a man in his forties stood up on one of the chairs in the sanctuary. If you've ever seen the movie The Karate Kid, you might remember the karate position called "The Crane." This is what he was doing as he stood on the chair shrieking. I told the church not to worry and went up to him and commanded the demon to come out. The man collapsed to the floor, was taken to an office, and there delivered.

There were so many counseling appointments where words of knowledge, words of wisdom, prophetic words, and deliverance worked all at the same time. One Thursday morning a man came to see me, and as usual I started with prayer. Within a few moments I heard this man chanting. I looked up, and he was sitting in a lotus position chanting his mantra. Then his entire face turned into a snout of a wolf. By the grace of God and power of Jesus' name though, his face returned to normal, and he was delivered.

Early another morning I got a call from the youth leader who had received a call from a mother of a boy in her youth group. The 17-

year-old boy was lying in his bed unresponsive, his eyes rolled back, unable to move. He was also grunting. I arrived at the home, and the youth leader, mother, and I went into his bedroom. We knelt to pray, and as soon as the words came out of our mouths, they hit the floor. There was no anointing. Nothing was happening; you could literally feel the room becoming void of the presence of God. The youth leader was feeling the same thing. I turned to his mother and said, "You're struggling with this." She responded that she was, and I asked her to leave the room the same way Jesus had people leave the house in Luke 8:54. He had to remove unbelief.

As soon as she left the room the glory of God literally filled it. The young man began to thrash back and forth as we prayed. His grunting got louder. God told me that in his closet there was a box full of occult tapes. We put them out of the house, and the thrashing got worse. The Lord then told me that there was a tape under his pillow. As I took it out the demon uttered a name, at which point I took the audio tape and snapped it in half, which is not humanly possible. Within a few minutes the young man was sitting up and in his right mind.

There was an evening I was called to go to someone's home, where a young woman was being demonized. As we began to pray, the woman began to scream. Perhaps 30 minutes went by, and there was a knock at the door. It was the police asking us what was going on. We were honest and told them that we were bringing this woman through deliverance. They both replied that they'd seen inexplicable things, like a man picking up an eight-foot couch with one hand and then throwing it and another man they couldn't subdue with even three tasers. They then left but requested that we try to be quieter.

Another night during a bible study a woman was continually interrupting me. I heard the Lord tell me to tell her that this was the night God was going to deliver her. She didn't say another word. After the study was over there remained the host couple, this woman, her husband, and myself. The woman weighed about 215 pounds and was a little over five feet tall. As I stood up and was perhaps two feet from her, I raised my right hand. I said, "In the name of Jesus," and as soon as I said that, a man's voice came out of the woman, the hair on my arms stood up, and I thought that then was a good time to leave the house.

Suddenly, though, there was a faith that rose up within me. I raised my hand again and said, "In the name of Jesus," and at that moment this woman was picked up and thrown about 15 feet in the air and then came crashing down to the floor. I didn't know how to pray so began speaking in tongues. The demon started shouting, "Stop that, stop that!" Paul tells us that, "though we speak with the tongues of men and of angels," the idea being that angels/demons can understand an angelic language if we are using one (1 Corinthians 13:1). Within a few minutes the woman sat up and didn't recall anything that had happened.

One night about 11 o'clock I was getting ready for bed and was just coming out of the shower when the phone rang. The young man who I had been training told me that he was at a woman's home with her husband and that the cupboards were opening and shutting all by themselves and the toilet seat going up and down. I told him to tell the demon to stop, and he said he'd tried that. He was experiencing a man's voice coming out of a woman and just didn't know what to do. Again, I told him to tell the demon to leave, and he told me that it wouldn't.

I believe it's important that we should mentor and train others to be ministers. We see this principle in Ephesians 4:11-12, *"And He Himself gave some to be apostles, some prophets, some evangelists, and some pastors and teachers, for the equipping of the saints for the work of ministry, for the edifying of the body of Christ."*

I was irritated at the enemy so got into my car and drove to the couple's home, which was not too far away. When I walked into the house, their dog came toward forward to bite me, and I realized that dogs too can be demonized. I rebuked the spirit in the dog, and it ran behind their couch and vomited a green substance. I have no idea what it was, but I'd seen this happen one morning at a church service when a demon was expelled from a young woman.

I went over to the woman sitting in the chair of her home and I said, "I'm not going to talk to you; I am going to talk to the demon." I told the demon it had to leave, and the demon left. I prayed with the couple and then went home to bed.

There are multiple stories that I could tell, but I believe that you've heard enough accounts to illustrate how awesome and powerful is the love and affection and power of God.

The Power of God One Afternoon

I remember one afternoon I traveled to a home in Fairhaven, Massachusetts where I used to run a 40-person cell group. Once in a while I would travel there during the day to also do some counseling.

It was one afternoon after walking into the home where the home group met, that the host said to me that their dog was very sick and they were told he would likely not live much longer. (This was an older dog.) As I walked into the living room the dog came over to greet me. Instead of petting the dog, however, I laid hands on the beautiful golden retriever and prayed. As I did, the dog's legs spread out in a way I didn't think possible, and the dog went out in the spirit. He literally fell and what we would say, "fell asleep." I had never seen anything like this. The dog eventually got up and yes, lived for many years after that.

After praying for the dog, I walked into the kitchen where I sat around a kitchen table consoling people. As I walked into the kitchen two of the stovetop kitchen burners literally exploded. I mean there were two loud explosions, and flames and sparks flew everywhere.

To this day I have no idea what happened and why it happened, except that perhaps God wanted to demonstrate to me that His anointing on each of us is very real. I said "on us" because all of us carry an anointing as His sons and daughters. 1 John 2:20 (NKJV): *"But you have an anointing from the Holy One, and you know all things."* Verse 27 says, *"But the anointing which you have received from Him abides in you."* We all have received an anointing, and it is not only on us, but in us.

The homeowners didn't mind that their stove elements had blown up. They were so ecstatic that God had not only healed their dog, but extended his life many for years.

God Provides a Vacation

Somewhere around 1986 the Holy Spirit had been speaking to me for months about going away to be alone with Him. My wife and I hadn't been on vacation for years, so I was thinking that there was no way I could tell her this. It was during a Thursday evening service however, when Pastor Tony (the senior pastor of Christian Life Fellowship), stood up and remarked to the church that he'd been away a lot and that I'd meanwhile been there holding down the fort. He went on to say that he felt the congregation should bless me so that I could go away for a weekend to New Hampshire. There might have been 100 people in the service that night, and people just came up to me and started cramming money into my hand and pockets. I went home with over $1,500.

With that kind of blessing we looked at going to Florida for a week, but discovered that it was cheaper to go to the Bahamas. It took us a couple of months to clear our schedules, but when they were open, off Donna and I went. We had never had a honeymoon, and now God was providing one!

When we returned from our weeklong stay in the Bahamas, the woman who was babysitting our children came to me and said that every time she passed the brown lazy boy chair in our basement, she felt God's presence. I told her that that was where I prayed every day. She added that she believed the Lord told her to tell me that I was supposed to go away. I didn't say anything to my wife, and we went to church that Sunday morning.

I was in the sanctuary when a very strange-looking woman approached me and said, "I believe the Lord wants you to go away to be alone with Him." Sadly, at different times we all fall into the trap of "judging a book by its cover." It is unfortunate that we see people as being strange rather than unique. One attitude reveals judgment, the other appreciation. Though I thought she was peculiar looking, I was stunned that she was adding to the confirmation of the Lord wanting me to go away.

Time for More Healing

When I got home I told my wife. She was very happy for me and wholeheartedly accepted the two messages I had received. Once again it took me a couple of months to clear my calendar, but I was finally able to free up some time to get away.

The night before I was going to leave, my wife asked me where I was headed, and I told her that I had no idea. Then at that moment I began to cry uncontrollably, just weeping and weeping. As I was crying, the thought came to me that perhaps I was supposed to go back to where I had grown up.

The next morning, I drove my car to the church to get a few things. My secretary asked me where I was going, and again, I broke into an uncontrollable bout of crying. She had never seen me cry like that, so she ran from the office to find the senior pastor and his wife. After I finished praying with them I got into my car and headed down route 118 from Rehoboth to Attleboro, Massachusetts. As I entered Attleboro I saw a baseball field on route 118 that I had played on when I was in the sixth grade.

Driving beside this baseball field I remembered its name. I hadn't thought about it for years and years. I felt I was to drive back to all the fields I'd played on, so I did. I drove to the next field, and as it was early in the morning, no one was there. All of a sudden, I had an open vision where I saw a championship baseball game I played in when I was in the sixth grade. I remembered that I was playing shortstop and all the bases were loaded. I was hoping the ball didn't come to me, but sure enough, the ball was hit directly to me.

By the time the ball reached me, the runner was almost at home plate. I threw the ball home, and the runner scored easily, at which point the coach came out and started yelling at me. It so affected me I never played baseball with confidence again. I remembered the coach's name. I forgave, released, and blessed him and his family. I then did the same for my father who never bothered to attend my athletic events.

I restarted my car and headed towards the center of Attleboro. I asked the Lord where he wanted me to go next. I could see that my knuckles were white as I was gripping the steering wheel of my car. I was angry. The thought came to my mind that I should go to the church that I had attended from the sixth through the eighth grades. The closer I got to the church, however, the angrier I became. In the brief time that I attended this particular congregational church I never once remember hearing the gospel preached. I heard a lot of philosophy, even psychology, but never the simple gospel truth that Jesus died for our sins.

As I pulled into the parking lot and got out of my car I looked for an open door. Each door I tried was locked, and I became increasingly angry because I knew that somebody was inside. I finally found a hidden door, one that was tucked away and not easily accessed, and went inside. I wanted to go into the sanctuary, but I found that the door had a very large chain that kept it locked and prohibited people from entering. My anger rose. I hear the sound of typing. (This was before the days of the computer.) I headed towards the sound and met the secretary, introducing myself as Reverend Brian Weeks. This was a very traditional church, so the term "Reverend" was appropriate. I told her I had attended the church as a youth and would appreciate the opportunity to go into the sanctuary.

As I stood in the middle of the sanctuary I wanted to curse the church because they didn't preach the gospel. As I was about to do that, however, I heard the Lord tell me to bless the church instead. So, I raised my hand and with a very loud voice began praying a blessing on the church. I even began praying in tongues. (Later I found out that while I was doing this the janitor was in the choir loft watching me.)

As I was standing there I felt God calling me into the reading room. (It is common for congregational churches to have designated rooms outside of the sanctuary for people to sit and read.) As I walked in I saw a bookrack and heard it calling to me. As I approached it, I heard a particular book say to me, "Pick me up and read me." I grabbed the book and opened to one of the pages, and words just seemed to jump off the page. I knew these words were for me. I read, "Sometimes in order to go forward you have to go backwards," which was exactly what I was doing that day. I had felt stuck and knew that I had to get unstuck but didn't know that going backwards would be part of it, that by doing so God could bring some healing. I needed the healing to allow me to go forward.

(A postscript to this story became evident around 1995. I was speaking to the town manager in Middleboro, Massachusetts where I had planted my first solo church, and he mentioned that he'd also attended the same congregational church. He told me that three years earlier God had sent a bible-believing pastor to this church, my prayer thus answered.)

I left the church and drove directly to the junior high that I attended while I lived in Attleboro. I had never driven there myself but knew exactly where to go. As I sat beside the school I thought of the principal as well as one of the teachers who seemed to always pick on me. Sitting in my car I forgave, released, and blessed the principal and then the teacher. By this point in time I was feeling sorry for myself and felt that I was supposed to drive to the elementary school that I attended when I was in the sixth grade. Again, I didn't know how to get there but managed to drive directly to the school.

It was school vacation, and I parked beside the field where we used to have recess. There was no one on the field, and now I had another open vision. I could see that it was recess time, and we were picking teams to play softball. I was always one of the captains and saw myself on one occasion picking my various teammates. The end of the process came where there were a few students who hadn't been picked yet. I said, "I don't want them." It became clear to me that I had continually put them down, rejected them, and spoken against them.

I began to cry, realizing that I had affected lives and families for generations. I thanked the Lord that He had already forgiven me. I started to pray for the lives of the people whom I had cursed with my voice and spoken against and asked God to bless them and their families and to bless their children and their grandchildren.

By this point I was feeling pretty crummy about myself.

I now felt led to drive around to the front of the school and park in the lot. I heard, "Go into the school." I tried to reason with God and tell him that the school was closed and no one was there. But that's an argument that you just don't win when you're talking to the Lord. I got out of my car, trying one door and then another, until I finally walked up the steps and saw that another door was open. I pulled it open and went inside.

Once inside I saw a janitor working in one of the offices. I asked him if I could look around, telling him that I had attended school there. As I walked down the hallway and looked into a classroom I had another vision. I could see a teacher yelling at me for no apparent reason, so I forgave her, released her, and blessed her, even blessing her family. I then looked into the next classroom and sure enough, there was another teacher yelling at me in the same manner. I blessed and released her and also blessed her family.

I was again feeling sorry for myself and felt I was being called to the gymnasium down the hallway. When I got there, I realized that this was a place I had vowed a vow that needed to be broken. Here in this gym I had declared the air around me cooler than any other place. It had been here where school dances and other events were held that my popularity was defined and I had cursed myself with pride. This had had a crippling effect on my life, my lifelong Achilles heel. How incredible years later to have the opportunity to break the vow in the spot I had made it.

I asked the Lord where I should go next, and He instructed me to go to the house where I had lived in Attleboro. I drove to the house and sat there feeling the Lord tell me to knock on the door and go inside. I was thinking, "I'm not going to do that. I'm not going to ring the doorbell." I had lived there for 26 years, so I drove away.

As I was leaving I saw the mailbox of a family who had been there when I lived in that neighborhood. I got out of my car and rang the doorbell. Sure enough, the woman answered the door, and I introduced myself. She asked me how my parents were, and in the conversation, I told her that I really wanted to visit the home that I had grown up in. She said that I probably could because the people who'd bought my parents' house still lived there. I got into my car, drove up to the house, and rang the doorbell.

The woman who had bought our house answered the door. She asked me if I would like to come in, and I said that I would. As we stood in the hallway I had a vision of the times when my mother had her mental breakdowns. I started seeing how painful a time it was and asked God to heal the memories that I was having. We went to the kitchen. There in the kitchen some other breakdowns occurred. Standing there I continued to have an open vision and was able to forgive, release, and bless.

I really wanted to go the glass-enclosed patio where I knew there'd been another mental breakdown. The woman just happened to invite me there. I went out there and was talking to her but was also praying, God fulfilling the word He had given me that morning: in order to go forward I needed to go backwards.

After this I asked where I was to go next, and I heard to Foxboro where I had grown up. I drove there and parked outside the home I had grown up in and where there were many memories that needed healing. I drove through the neighborhood in my car praying, forgiving, releasing, and blessing for all the incidents that had occurred while growing up there.

When I was done I asked the Lord where I should go from there. The Lord told me to drive to Walpole to the house where I had given my life to Jesus, and so I did. I drove there and parked outside the house where I had committed my life to Christ. I sat there thanking God first for His mercy, His grace, and His great compassion. From there I felt I was to call my former next-door neighbor who was a young man with whom I had gone to college. This was before the days of cell phones, so I had to go and find a payphone.

I spent the next two hours calling every Johnson in the phonebook. After two plus hours I was tired and frustrated and said to the Lord, "I thought you wanted me to talk to Jeff." The Lord asked me if Jeff was a friend of mine, and I answered yes. The Lord then told me that I didn't cherish relationships the way I should. The Holy Spirit was right; I certainly didn't cherish relationships because I'd been such a loner all my life, something I'm still working on today. I finally got Jeff's phone number after the Lord told me to call his father. I called Jeff and we chatted briefly. It turned out that he was a pastor in a Methodist church.

Since I was in Walpole I felt led to visit an Assembly of God church which I'd heard a lot about. I drove there and went into the sanctuary, where I walked to the altar area and prayed. My prayer was like talking to the walls. I was thinking to myself, "Well, I must've missed this one. I shouldn't have come." As I was leaving the church, however, I noticed a gymnasium on the property. I went to check it out, and a woman greeted me at a desk. She was checking to make sure that only members came in.

I introduced myself as Pastor Brian, and she let me in. As I was leaving, this same woman stopped me and said, "I've only done this once, maybe twice in my life, but I believe I'm supposed to say something to you." I told her that I was very open to hearing from God through other people. With that she said to me, "Sometimes in order to go forward, you have to go backwards." Amazingly she spoke the word word-for-word from the book, the exact phrase that I had read earlier that morning. The Holy Spirit was clearly speaking to me about what He wanted to accomplish on this two-day journey.

Divine Confrontation

I was then led to go and see an old friend for a time of confrontation. He and I had started a church together in Mansfield, Massachusetts after we had left the Worldwide Church of God. We named it The Church of God of Mansfield, and in a very short time there were about 75 people attending. Within just a few months of planting the church, however, I realized that God had not called us to start it. It was something that we had done on our own. I told Roland at the time that we weren't qualified to pastor a church that God had not called us to start. I told him I was leaving and never went back. I realized that just because something grows, it doesn't mean that God is in it.

I stopped in to see what he was doing. Within a very few minutes he expressed to me that he and the 13 people with him were the only ones in the world who had the truth. I never saw him again. He went on to become a cult leader of a group in Attleboro that got a lot of publicity following the death of one of the member's children, a child who happened to be Roland's grandson. How tragic!

As I look back on this I am so thankful for the leading of the Holy Spirit. You have to think where I'd be today if I hadn't heard

God's voice about our not being qualified. It causes me to say, "Father, thank you."

Can I encourage all of you to cultivate a desire and willingness to hear God's voice such that you allow Him to correct/adjust and direct your steps? After all, correction is not condemnation. Jacques, Roland's son, is now serving life in prison for the death of that child.

This summer I saw Bob and Judy Pardon of Meadowhaven, a ministry in Lakeville, MA which ministers to cult victims. Bob and Judy were expert witnesses in Jacques' trial yet have since formed a very close relationship with him in prison. I asked Bob and Judy if my wife Donna and I could see him, and they responded with a wholehearted "Yes!" We hope to make time to do so later this year. [1]

After visiting Roland in North Attleboro, I drove to my parents' home in Norton because I wanted to finally confront them about some things in my childhood. As I drove into the driveway, I was expecting to see my father's car, but it wasn't there. Instead I was surprised to see one of my sister's vehicles. I went inside and asked her to wake up my mother from the nap she was taking. Though my sister tried for several minutes, she was unsuccessful, and it became clear that God didn't want me to confront my parents over my childhood. I was to instead let things go, which I did. While I was there my sister asked me what I'd been doing for the

---

[1] Anne, who is editing this book and who also worked on my first book Musings, told me that she and her husband Ken have known and supported Bob and Judy for years. They are intimately aware of the story: the cult, the trial, and the tragedy of Jacques' imprisonment. Both Ken and Anne were amazed at God's grace in warning me AND the grace of my *hearing*!

entire day. I told her, and then God give me a word of knowledge about her life. The whole thing was really powerful.

Before leaving my parents' house I asked the Lord whether or not I was supposed to go home. I heard Him say, "No. I want you to go to Mansfield and stay at the Days Inn." Number one, I do not like Mansfield. Number two, I don't like Days Inns, and number three, I didn't know if there even <u>was</u> a Days Inn in Mansfield. After finding a copy of the yellow pages, I discovered that there was indeed a Days Inn there, so I called and made a reservation.

I then left my parents' house and drove to my brother's. I wanted to see him, because he was going blind in both eyes due to contact he'd had with unusual bacteria. When I arrived, our conversation didn't go very well, but the wonderful news since then is that we have become extremely close. It's truly been a real blessing to have him and his family in my life.

God Waits in a Hotel Room

After leaving my brother's home I drove to the Days Inn in Mansfield. It was about 8:30 as I was checking in, and I was emotionally exhausted. I took the elevator up and slid in the card key, and the door opened. As it opened it appeared that somebody had left the light on near the bed, although I couldn't tell because the entrance to the space was very narrow, and I couldn't see that far. I was a few feet into the room when I saw the glory of God hovering over the bed. Imagine walking into a room, and the shekinah glory of God has filled a quarter of it!

I went and sat on the bed for over two hours. I had to go to the bathroom, but I was afraid if I did, the glory would leave the room. I finally had no choice, so as fast as I could I went in and out of the bathroom. God's literal presence was still there. During those two hours, I didn't say anything nor did He. There was really nothing to say; there was simply the unspeakable joy of being in His presence. I sat up against the bed's headboard for another couple of hours.

It was time to get into the bed, but I first needed to take a shower. Again, I was afraid that if I did, God would leave the room. I finally decided to take the fastest shower in my life, and thankfully, He didn't leave. I got in bed and fell asleep sitting up against the headboard, never uttering or hearing a word.

When I woke up the next morning the shekinah glory of God was gone, but there was a cloud in my room. I asked the Lord if I could spend the day there in a hotel with Him just enjoying His presence. He told me I had to leave the hotel because there was more He wanted to do. I spent the next hour trying to convince Him that I should be able to stay in the hotel all day, and He could work on me there.

God Waits for Me in a Retreat Center and Book Store

I checked out and then felt the Lord telling me to drive to Sharon, Massachusetts to a center where I had conducted some retreats. I walked in, and they remembered me. I told them that I was there to pray.

I went into the sanctuary and began to pray. It was cold, but the heat couldn't be turned up. I prayed and I prayed. I lay on the altar and prayed. I prayed every way you can think of to get God's attention. For two and a half hours I prayed. Finally, I sat down and put my head into my hands. I was tired and frustrated that God wasn't saying anything. As soon as I was quiet I heard God say to me. "Are you done?"

I knew exactly what He was talking about. He just wanted me to come and sit and be quiet. When I finally quieted myself, the Holy Spirit did a download about prophetic ministry. It was incredible, because I had never read anything on the topic. In fact, at this time there wasn't a whole lot that was being written about it. The download ended, and it was time to go home. On the way, I felt like God told me to stop at a Christian bookstore in Plainville.

Because I thought that the idea was crazy, I drove past the exit that I should have taken for the bookstore. God insisted I turn around, take the next exit, and go back. I didn't know where it was but ended up driving right to the front door. God simply said take this turn, then that one. I had no idea where I was going, but God did.

I walked in and just started looking around. In a few minutes, I saw the same book I had seen the day before in the reading room of the congregational church. What are the odds of that happening? I found another book which I ended up purchasing, and that book has shaped much of my attitude about being a prophetic person.

At this point I was headed home but was told to stop and get something to eat so I could bring the first book with me to read. As I was sitting in this restaurant I began the book called "The Elijah Task." As I started reading I began to reading exactly what God had downloaded at the retreat center. I didn't have to remember what he had said to me earlier. He gave me a book to remind me!

I arrived home to a loving and understanding wife. I can't begin to tell you all the times she has been there for me as I pursued God, or rather, God has pursued me. For 45 years she has stood with me over and over again, always supporting me and when appropriate, lovingly challenging me about certain decisions and asking me why I was making them. As you can imagine after reading this book, all during these years Donna has had to have her own relationship with God and faith in Him. If you ever see her by the way, please commend her for being an amazing woman.

God Shows Up at a Christian School Chapel

In my 11 years at Christian Life I was the associate pastor, the house prophet, and the principal of the Christian school. As the principal of the school I would lead chapel every morning, and during a number of them God would just show up. There was this one morning when the presence of God was so incredible that all day we never left the chapel. Every single student there was touched powerfully by God. Some were crying and praying with one another, and you would see at different times students falling under His power.

We didn't even stop to have lunch. In fact, when the parents arrived at 2:30 to pick up their children, they couldn't because God's anointing was still moving; many of the students were still lying on the floor under the His power. In retrospect, I recall many chapels during which God would manifest His presence in a similar way.

The Jericho Years

The Holy Spirit Instructs Me to Take a Drive

In 1989, I had a deep desire to leave and plant my own church, but there was no release from the Lord to do so. So, from 1989 to 1992 I continued to serve faithfully and wait for the Lord to tell me when I could leave.

It was the early spring of 1992, and I had just finished a 21-day fast. It was not uncommon for me to fast for long periods of time just for the purpose of drawing close to the Lord, and on one particular Saturday morning the Holy Spirit said to me, "Today I will show you where you will start a church." I went to Donna and asked her if she wanted to go for a ride. She said, "I know that look on your face. You go for the ride and tell me what God shows you, and I will do whatever He tells you."

I got into my car and went to the end of our street. I made a very smart decision by asking the Lord which direction to go. I would have turned right, because for the last 15 years the people in this direction knew me and my ministry. But God being God, I was instructed to turn left. I traveled two miles to the intersection of route 44 and route 118. I would've turned left because again, in that direction people knew me and knew my ministry, but instead God had me turn right.

I traveled about eight or nine miles until I entered the city of Taunton. At the Taunton green, there is a rotary where the road splits in several directions. There at the rotary I simply asked which way God wanted me to go. I felt Him say that I should go straight. I continued to travel down route 44 all the while hoping that God would not show me to start a church in Taunton, because I was not fond of the city at the time. After I drove through Taunton I come to the town of Raynham. I really like Raynham so began looking at all the vacant stores that were available on route 44, but God told me to keep on traveling, so I did.

At this point in time I crossed over Route 24 and headed towards Middleboro and Plymouth. I was now about 30 miles from our home. I came to the rotary in Middleboro and again was faced with taking a left to Bridgewater, taking a slight left to Plymouth, or taking a right-hand turn to New Bedford. Which way do you want me to go, I asked. The answer was to go straight down route 28.

I traveled about a mile and came to a stop light. At that stop light on the right- hand side of the road was a small grassy area where there was a large brick cross about 12 to 14 feet high. On the cross, there were silver letters attached spelling the word "worship." At that point, the presence of God filled my car, and I had to pull over because I began crying uncontrollably. I was shaking, and my nose was running.

It was an incredible experience to have God sit with me in the car. I said to the Lord that while I really appreciated the experience, I really needed a word. Immediately I heard Acts 17:6. I had brought my Bible with me, and so I turned to Acts 17:6, and here is what it says, "These men have come to this city and they have turned it upside down." This prophetic word is exactly what God did in the years that followed, something I'll cover in my next chapter.

I returned home to tell my wife what had happened, and she said, "I'll go wherever you want to go, and we'll serve God together." At this point in time no one knew what had been on my heart for the last three years, not even my two best friends who were both on the board of elders. They had no idea that I was praying about starting my own church. I never told them and had never even hinted, so they literally had no idea.

On Monday morning, I went to see Pastor Tony and told him that I was going to resign and start my own church. It was quite a shock for him, so the conversation didn't go as well as I would've liked. We had an emergency elders' meeting where the credentialing committee that held his and my ordination credentials was invited to come and sit in our meeting. The purpose was to have them give us their perspective of my decision. They listened to what Pastor Tony had to say and also my thoughts and then went to his office to discuss the matter. When they returned they said they fully believed that I was to leave and start my own church.

For the next two months, we planned my exit. I continued to be the principal of the Christian school, and my responsibilities and duties were transitioned to Pastor Ron, who was on staff. The elders decided in a board meeting that they would not give me severance pay. So, I left with no money and no job, yet Donna and I had total trust that God would provide and the assurance that He was with us.

It was perhaps two, maybe three weeks later that I received a letter in the mail from the board of elders stating that they had reconsidered and had decided to pay me three month's severance. This was an amazing miracle.

We did not tell anyone even during the transition where we would be starting the church. I made a covenant promise with the board of elders that if anyone asked me where I was going I would not tell them, and I kept that promise. After the shocking announcement on a Sunday morning that I would be leaving, several people called me asking where I was going to plant a church. If they were attending Christian Life Fellowship I told them I wouldn't tell them because they already had a church. This was also true for others outside of Christian Life. If they already had a home church I told them that I wouldn't tell them my destination. I knew I was to plant a church in Middleboro but had no idea where and when.

My eleven years at Christian Life Fellowship were amazing. Our church grew and grew, and the Holy Spirit had assembled an amazing number of deacons and leaders. From Christian Life four other churches were birthed: Jericho Christian Fellowship, which has become LightHouse Church, Judah Christian Fellowship, which has become Gates of Praise Christian Fellowship, Solomon's Porch, and Master Builders Ministries. The church continues to this day under the leadership of Pastor Robert Bernier. Sadly, Pastor Tony was called home way too early, but his legacy continues on.

The Holy Spirit Starts a Church

My last Sunday at Christian Life was near the end of June 1992. I wasn't ready to go headlong into starting a church. I needed some alone time. I needed to spend some time asking the Lord about what kind of church He wanted me to plant, and I also needed a philosophy of ministry. Besides all this there was location: I had no idea where I would find a place that I could afford to rent.

It was during this period of time that I received some incredible news through the mail. Eleven years prior to this time I had gone to court to settle a workman's compensation case that I had been involved in years earlier. At the close of the case the judge said he would take it under advisement, which means he didn't know how to rule. While waiting for the ruling my attorney and the judge both died, so my case just sat. Eleven years later I got a letter stating that the new judge insisted they reach a settlement. They decided to give me $11,000 after the lawyer fees. Several times I had wanted that settlement, but God's timing was and is always perfect. God had waited to provide working capital and a safety net for my income. Once the church started it grew so rapidly that after three months there was just enough money coming in to support my salary.

I began taking day trips to Middleboro looking for a space to rent. There were very few places that were for rent, never mind with our unique needs. I made several trips to Middleboro, driving from one end to the other, an area covering 64 square miles. One of my trips had me cross the Middleboro/Lakeville town line. I found this awesome place about a thousand feet into Lakeville. It was beautiful-- lots of flexible space, air conditioning, abundant parking, new bathrooms. It was the perfect place. I loved it. It was not only affordable, but highly visible. There was only one small problem, however, and the Lord brought it to my attention. He said to me, "I didn't call you to Lakeville."

Ugh...

Now I was back to not having a clue where to find a place to start the church. As I was driving around a number of days later, I drove by a realtor's office in Lakeville. Even though it was in Lakeville I felt led to go in. Once inside I talked to a woman who told me that she had the perfect place in Middleboro which had been vacant for three years. She went on to say that it was located right on route 28, a heavily-traveled road.

I met with the owners who had a 3,000 square-foot building. They could rent half of it or the whole thing, and the price was reasonable. Now what do I do? By this time 17 people had committed to help me start this new church. I contacted them and asked them to meet me at this building. Everyone brought a folding chair. I shared my vision, which took about an hour and a half, while the people who were willing to rent the building sat in their truck.

At the end of my sharing I asked everyone to take a piece of paper and write down how much they gave to the Lord every week; not what they hoped to give, not what they wanted to give, but what they actually gave the Lord. I told them not to put their names on the paper, and so they didn't. We collected all the little pieces of paper, added them up, and discovered we could not even afford to rent half of the building. We left, and I thanked the people who had been waiting in the truck.

I went home and the next day and for the next week or longer my phone rang continually. People would call and say they heard I was starting a church, and again I would ask them what church they attended. The majority of them said that at the moment they didn't attend any church. I thanked them and said that as of that point I hadn't yet found a place to meet. To be honest I didn't put any credence into their inquiry; I just blew it off. But then the Lord spoke to me about beginning to write down all the people who had called me, and so I did and compiled a list of 68 people.

With that in mind I drove to Middleboro and met with Victor and Donna who were the owners of the building. I told them I wanted to rent the whole building but did not have the necessary first or last month's rent, or even the security deposit. I told them that in fact I had no money at all to give them. I then informed them that they needed to renovate the entire left side of the building where all the offices were, removing all of them in order to create an open space for our sanctuary. They looked at one another, and Victor said, "I don't know why, but I am going to do that for you."

I then contacted the 17 people and the others who'd called me. I told the original 17 that when we returned from our vacation we would work on the building together. My wife and I and our two children went to Montréal and had the most phenomenal vacation we'd ever had as a family -- it was just spectacular. We came back about a week later and drove to the church in Middleboro anticipating we'd have to clean and paint. When I walked into the building I discovered this wouldn't be necessary. The entire building had already been renovated, cleaned, and painted. The landlord had done everything.

We needed to purchase chairs and carpeting. A long-time friend offered to loan us $5,000 interest free so we could buy carpet and chairs for the sanctuary, and within a few days we had both. We decided to have church on Sunday morning. I had no idea how many people were going to come to this first church service but simply had the faith that God was going to provide.

I arrived early Sunday morning to ensure everything was in place and then went upstairs in the attic to pray with a handful of people. When ten o'clock came I walked downstairs to begin the service. I walked in the room and was shocked to find a room filled with 71 people. It was just so amazing. Out of the 71 there were 20 people who had come to wish me well and let me know they were not going to make Jericho their home but were nonetheless going to love and support me as best they could. That meant Jericho started with 50 people, many of whom drove an hour to come. This church held 150, and we outgrew it in a year and a half.

I had signed a three-year lease, but Victor and Donna were willing to let us out of it, as their oil business had increased over 50 percent in the short time we were there. By God's grace I knew a Lutheran Church that was meeting in the YMCA and approached the pastor to see if he would have any interest in renting the building we were leaving. Victor and Donna never missed a day's rent.

God Provides a New Place to Meet

Once again, we were in need of a new place to meet. I again drove all over the town of Middleboro looking for a place that would accommodate us. At one point, I even looked at some chicken coops in the southern part of town! Just down the road about a mile and a half from where we were meeting there was a beautiful building for lease. I called the owners, who wanted an astronomical amount of money. So, week after week I continued to look for a new place to meet.

One day as I was driving I noticed that the realtor's sign had been changed on the building that would accommodate us but which was too expensive. Because of the realtor change I called them, and they asked me to give them a proposal. My proposal involved a three-year escalation plan involving paying a certain amount one year, a second amount the second year, and the same amount for the third year. I also asked them to remodel the building.

I shouldn't have been surprised, but they came back and accepted my offer but were unwilling to remodel the building. I had an architect follow my design and a handful of us did the remodel. It turned out beautifully. Within a year we had grown again to the extent that we needed to expand the sanctuary and create a room for fellowship. Thankfully the building we were in had additional space we could afford to rent. Another year and a half went by, and we outgrew this building. At the same time, the building went into foreclosure, so either way we needed to do something quickly.

I took my normal town-wide tour of Middleboro only to find that there was really nothing available. I began looking at parcels of land to see what we could afford. I really loved the property directly behind where we were meeting and went to the town hall to see what I could find out. The information available did not provide the owner's name, as it was a private investor and no one knew how to contact him.

God Purchases Land and Builds a Building

Just prior to our family vacation in Michigan I met with the town manager with whom I had a relationship. I was telling him about my situation and how I couldn't find the owner of the property. He smiled and told me, "That's easy; he's a good friend of mine" and then asked me what I wanted to offer him for the land. I knew he had purchased the land 10 years earlier and paid $46,000, but now the property was worth close to a half million. I made the offer of $80,000 cash, and the balance of the worth I would give him as a charitable contribution.

Off we went to Michigan, and I was feeling pretty discouraged. While we were there the town manager called and told me that the owner of the property had accepted my offer. This was sometime during the early summer or towards the beginning of July. I periodically called the owner of the property and asked him to have the land appraised so we could give him a legal 501(c) (3) contribution receipt. He never returned my calls.

It was a couple days after Christmas when the attorney for the owner of the land called me and said they wanted to close on the land before the first of the year. I told him that I didn't have the $80,000, and he said not to worry about it, that I should just come and he would deed me the land. I drove to Walpole and with no money exchanged, they deeded the property into the church's name and gave me a check to pay the taxes on the land. I drove to Plymouth and for $35 registered the land in the church's name. Can you say miracle?

I began to design a building and then sent it out to get various quotes on the cost to build it. The average bid was a $1,200,000. At that point, I decided that I would subcontract the construction of the building myself. When we got all the bids back and after some negotiating, the entire cost of the building and land was $450,000. Can you say miracle?

During the process of design and bidding I had been talking to a local bank to secure a loan. They assured me that we could secure a construction loan, but I was about to leave for Israel. I called the bank to verify the fact that when I returned we could sign papers. When I spoke to the vice president with whom I had been negotiating, he informed me that the bank had changed its mind because we were an independent church with no parent organization willing to co-sign for us.

Once again, we were facing an obstacle, but I want to tell you that we serve the God who overcomes obstacles. I was feeling discouraged, but Jack Bradley, one of the key people in the founding and establishing of Jericho, worked closely beside me and had heard of a church bond company that loaned money to churches who didn't have parent organizations supporting them. I contacted the church bond company the day before I went to Israel and ended up faxing them three years- worth of our year-end statements.

Four days later I was in Israel on the Sea of Galilee, and my wife called me, which she would never do unless it was something extremely important. She told me that the church bond company had approved our application. I instructed her to contact Jack and the elders to hold a meeting with all the leaders of the church, as I understood that without the backing of the church leaders it wouldn't be possible to move forward. We needed the leadership to be behind us.

They held the meeting. I wasn't there, but the leadership unanimously decided to approve the selling of church bonds. When I returned from Israel we began selling the bonds, and within five weeks we had sold all but $80,000. Another miracle?

One of the most incredible things that God did around this time concerned the husband of a long-time member of our church. This woman deeply loved her husband and was forever trying to influence him to become a believer. We had perspectives printed, one of which she'd brought home and had sitting on the coffee table. Her husband picked it up, looked at it, and was amazed that a church would have this kind of business savvy. He decided to invest a very large sum of money. The most wonderful thing about that investment was that he also committed his life to Christ!

Upon my return from Israel we walked the land and found a very large hole on the property that would likely require us to purchase fill. This was especially concerning because the former owner of the land wanted to remove some loam and gravel from the site. I called him and requested that he kindly NOT remove so much gravel and loam off the site that we would have to import and pay for more. He told me to never mind, that I could keep the loam and gravel.

If you remember, we paid $80,000 for the land. We then sold $43,000 of gravel and loam, so the land only cost us $37,000. Not only that, but all the site excavation and building of a new road were done for free. We started excavation in May and moved into our brand-new building on Christmas Eve. He is indeed the God of miracles!

If you recall that when I was working at ADP I had become the credit manager. It was while working this job that I learned about the world of finances. Our Father has a way of training us for His purposes even when we don't realize that He is preparing us for our tomorrow!

God Adds an Addition and Staff

Within a couple of years, we were having two services but really wanted only one. It was decided we would put on a 5,000 square-foot addition, increasing the size of the sanctuary, and adding a fellowship room and multiple classrooms. It was an amazing addition.

It was a short time after we had finished the building addition that I became very tired of American Christian music. It was as if the artists were more interested in producing albums than trying to find the heart of God - production rather than anointing. The presence of God was being sacrificed so more songs could be produced. With that in mind I prayed and asked the Lord where his heart was in music. Very clearly, I heard him say "Australia." This was before Hillsong had become known in the United States. I responded to this word by faxing every charismatic church there.

In my fax, I said I believed that God had a new sound in Australia which He wanted to bring to America. Given that I requested that they be so kind as to send me copies of their music CDs and charts. Within a few weeks I got a fax back from a pastor named Glenn Feehan who was the worship leader of Christian City Church under Phil Pringle. Pastor Glenn told me that he was packing his family to come to America to bring a new song. When I received his fax, God showed me that he would be on our staff in the near future. With confidence, I pretended that Glenn was actually on staff and so weekly put away a salary for him in a savings account. While there were many weeks that we didn't have the money for this, I still believed we needed to activate what God had shown us.

Pastor Glenn arrived first in Dallas, Texas, and after nine months there I asked if he could bring his wife and family to Massachusetts. I wanted to meet his whole family, not just him. Glenn came with his wife Robyn who is also now a pastor, and their family, and there was definitely a supernatural connection. Shortly after Pastor Glenn returned to Texas we made him an offer to become part of our staff. The money we had had put aside we used to pay for his trip to Massachusetts from Texas. We also had the funds to pay for his initial rent and security for his new home in Plymouth. God moves in so many diverse ways. I hope you are seeing how much of a miracle all of this was.

Before Glenn arrived, we knew that we would have to expand at some point in time. With this in mind we wanted to buy the land that was next to us. We had asked the owner how much he wanted for the parcel of land, but his asking price was too much money, more money than the land was worth. Within the year, however, the owner of the property called us and said he was willing to sell the land for half the cost and that he would hold the mortgage with no money down.

On the parcel of land that we had purchased was a motorcycle shop. The shop owner wanted to buy less than a quarter acre of property, which we ended up selling him for an incredible amount. We also sold gravel and loam from the land we had purchased. With all these things God was giving us the ability to increase the size of our property and thus prepare for the future.

Within less than a year the son of the man who had sold us the property and also owned a house abutting it, wanted us to purchase his home, and we did. It was around the same time that we decided that we needed to hire another person to be our community pastor and evangelist. We hired Pastor Lauren, and he moved into the home we had purchased.

Lauren started a program called Jairus Agency. Perhaps you remember the story of Jairus and his daughter? Jairus had died, and everybody thought it was hopeless that Jesus could bring her back to life. This hopelessness was similar to the attitude that many people had towards drug-addicted young people - that it was impossible for them to turn their lives around. Most of them had been kicked out of school due to zero tolerance policies. They needed community service, yet with none being offered, the Jairus program stepped in, enabling records to be wiped clean. We found schools for these young men and women, and every one of them graduated from high school and the majority of them from college as well.

It wasn't too long after we hired Lauren that we sold the house he had been living in and a small portion of the land. With the funds, we purchased land downtown and built a community center called the HUB. To help offset the small mortgage we had on the property, we built two apartments above the community center.

At the HUB, we offered a program for children who had difficulty reading. In addition, we offered anger management, character development for young women, and a host of other programs. We also developed a program which involved a number of churches sending their benevolence money. People seeking benevolence would be screened and would have to meet a certain set of criteria. This meant that a person couldn't go from church to church seeking assistance.

Within the first year of Jericho being planted, I wrote the town manager and said that when civil authorities and spiritual authorities gather for prayer, God moved in those communities. The letter was sent to the head of every department in the town. The town manager took me up on it and the selectmen on a few occasions. The meetings with the town manager were regular, and he and his wife even became active in our church.

You might recall that the word God gave me when I first came to Middleboro was "These men have come to this city and turned it upside down." God is willing to fulfill His word that he speaks to each of us and is looking for men and women who are willing to stand in the gap (Ezekiel 22:30).

God Chooses a Name

It's important that I go back and tell you how Jericho Christian Fellowship got its name. One night before we had our first service I was kneeling and praying in my office. The Lord said to me, "You never asked me about the name of the church." I had been planning to name the church Middleboro Christian Fellowship and asked Him what he thought of it. He said "No." I asked Him what His name for it would be, and without any hesitation I heard "Jericho."

I paused for a moment and told Him that Jericho was a stupid name. I couldn't even say it. Who wants to build a church that is going to fall?! There was a moment of silence before I heard the Lord say to me, "Look up what the word Jericho means." I told Him I could do that and proceeded to look it up in Hebrew. Turns out that the word Jericho means "fragrance." I was totally blown away, because my entire philosophy of ministry revolved around that concept. I had written that a sacrificed life was a fragrance to the Lord, that worship was a fragrance to the Lord, that our giving financially was a fragrance to the Lord and serving was a fragrance to the Lord. The Holy Spirit had summarized everything I wanted the church to be in one word.

Indeed, we had the presence of God in each and every service. It was incredible. I will share just a few of the miraculous things we saw God do.

Miraculous Events

We had a Sunday evening service where God was moving in prayer. A woman pastor from Pittsburg was in attendance who was totally blind. She had been at our Sunday morning service and had received prayer. At some point, she went into the bathroom, and one of our college-age women went in at the same time. There in the bathroom the young woman felt led to pray for the blind pastor. A short time later this blind woman pastor began to yell that she could see, and as each minute passed her sight improved. Before we began telling the world that God had restored her sight however, we asked her to make an appointment with a doctor to review all her medical records. Indeed, when God does something, it can stand the test. Sure enough, the next day she saw an eye doctor and after seeing all her records, he verified that God had restored her sight!

One Sunday morning when we were worshipping the fire alarm went off. As we looked up we saw all around us that inside our 22 plus-foot ceiling, a blue-tinted cloud had covered the entire sanctuary. The cloud was about eight feet deep. The fire alarm went off, and we had to exit the building and wait for the fire department to come. When the fire department arrived, they ascended straight to our attic. In the attic, the cloud was very thick, like a dense fog. They had all their instruments that measure various levels of smoke properties, yet nothing was registering on their meters. They had no doubt, however, that there was a cloud of smoke in our building. The cloud was much like the shekinah cloud of glory described in scripture (Exodus 16:10).

Finally, one of the firemen said that while he didn't know what it was, it was safe to be there. I spoke to the firemen in the attic and said to them that I knew what it was, that it was the presence of God. One of them responded, "Well I don't know what it is, but it's real." The fire department then told everyone they could re-enter the building, and we spent the entire rest of the service worshipping. The next day one of the contractors we used was walking through the sanctuary when he stopped and said, "Do you know that you have a cloud in your building?"

On another Sunday morning, we were worshipping and it began to rain inside of the building. Big droplets of water hit the pages of our Bibles and those same water droplets were causing our arms to get wet. As suddenly as the rain started, it stopped.

Close to Thanksgiving we decided to bring a number of churches together for a night of joint worship which we held at Middleboro High School. Somewhere in the middle of the service it started to rain, but it was raining only in the front row. In the morning, it had also rained in the sanctuary, but throughout the whole room instead of just in the front.

We had several prophetic meetings each year where people were supernaturally spoken to by God. Lives were healed and transformed with just a few words.

Gideon Revival

Speaking of prophetic meetings, I want to share about the most powerful prophetic service I have ever attended.

In the early 2000s we invited Fergus McIntyre, a prophet from Australia, to come and minister for four days. At the first meeting Fergus stood up and said there was no anointing to prophesy, at which point I stood up and commended him for not prophesying.

The second meeting we held had over 450 people in attendance. Within the first five minutes Fergus said he felt "naughty," which is an expression used by those from Australia and New Zealand when they feel like the anointing is on them and they're unsure of how to proceed. At this point, there were a number of people who had to stand because there weren't enough chairs. Fergus walked up to someone who was standing, took his Bible, and tapped the person on the forehead. As soon as contact was made, the person fell to the ground under the power of God.

Fergus proceeded to tap everyone on the forehead. When the people went down they didn't get up for several minutes. The entire sanctuary was littered with bodies, and there was no more room for people to fall. We went into the foyer and past the church offices, past the nursery, and the bathrooms, and back into the sanctuary. I believe Fergus prayed for everyone with the exception of a few people who didn't want it. Out of everyone he prayed for, there was only one person who didn't fall under the power of God.

It was one of those meetings that created controversy. Yet I believe in the power of God which Paul speaks of in 1 Corinthians 2:4 (NKJV) *"And my speech and my preaching were not with persuasive words of human wisdom, but in demonstration of the Spirit and of power."* That Sunday we lost 43 families. People told me if Fergus came back that they would leave. I told them it looked like they'd be leaving. When you believe in something you cannot allow the opinions of others to steal it.

Interestingly, though we lost many families, our church income was not affected.

Time to Plant Another Church

In 1995 the Lord spoke to me about starting another church, because He wanted church planting to be part of Jericho's DNA. I asked the Lord where he wanted to plant a church, and His response was "Fall River." I asked him why. He spoke to me from the book of Exodus where the children of Israel cry out because of their bondage. God said to me, "Do you hear their cry?" Exodus 3:7 (NKJV) says, *"And the Lord said: 'I have surely seen the oppression of My people who are in Egypt, and have heard their cry because of their taskmasters, for I know their sorrows.'"*

Immediately I was able to hear the cry of the hurting and the broken in the city. The Lord went on to show me Isaiah 61:1-2, that one of the purposes of the anointing is to heal the broken-hearted. Isaiah 61:1-2: *"The Spirit of the Lord God is upon Me, Because the Lord has anointed Me to preach good tidings to the poor; He has sent Me to heal the brokenhearted, to proclaim liberty to the captives, And the opening of the prison to those who are bound; To proclaim the acceptable year of the Lord."*

He went on to show me that the hurting and the broken weren't welcomed in many of the churches in the city. He wanted them to have a place where they could go to find healing, dignity, honor, and value, a place where they could become sons and daughters of the most-high God.

Over the next number of weeks, I mused with the Lord about this church. The Lord told me that the name of the church should be called Judah Christian Fellowship. Very clearly the Holy Spirit gave me a three-year plan to follow. I was to plant and establish the church in year one; in year two I was to continue to establish the church and to look for someone to take the church over, and year three would be the year of transition during which I would transfer the church to someone else.

We held our first meeting, and I had a particular elder from Jericho who I was hoping would be able to take over the church in its third year. Unfortunately, that didn't work out. It was during this first year that another pastor from the city who had a small church began attending Judah. He had the same vision for the city, the hurting, and the broken. In fact, the name of his church was called Gates of Praise. You can see that even the meaning of the church names was the same.

After the first year I was very tired, as I was pastoring a church in Middleboro and was ministering every Sunday night in this new church in Fall River. Because I was tired and weary I made a very poor decision.

Clearly, I was given a three-year plan, but my exhaustion caused my flesh to transfer the church early in the second, instead of the third year. Pastor Don Boucher and his wife took the church over in the second year, and I'm thankful to tell you that the church still exists today in downtown Fall River.

Our God is so gracious and so kind that even when we make bad decisions He doesn't abandon us. Even with that being true, if I had to do it again I would obviously not make the same mistake. The Lord will always lead us and He'll show us what to do; it just requires one simple thing - our obedience.

Time to Move On

I started Jericho in June 1992 and then in late September 2008 I went on a medical sabbatical. The back problems I had been healed of in 1981 had been troubling me for the past seven years. In 2001 while vacationing in Florida, the lounge chair I was sitting on folded in half, and I was thrown onto the patio deck near the pool. Immediately I knew that something was wrong, so I went to the emergency room, and after several appointments over a number of months it was decided that the scar tissue that was holding my vertebrae in place was torn. After the removal of my disc I had a natural fusion, and the scar tissue was interfering with my nerve canal.

For seven years I tried to live with the pain, but in the end, I was taking too much medication, and it really affected my leadership. It was decided I should take a sabbatical to get well. While on sabbatical the elders felt that they wanted to take the church in a different direction and decided to replace me as the senior pastor. Rather than bring the church through tremendous turmoil, it became clear that it was time for me to let go of the church. The Holy Spirit has very unique ways of moving us on and creating dramatic change in our lives. We often don't recognize what God is doing however, because our heart and emotions cloud our ability to see. This was one example.

Solomon's Porch: God Names the Church

In December 2009, the Lord spoke to me about taking the home meeting we were enjoying and making it public. While we were meeting in a home there was no need for a name, but now that we needed one, I called it Solomon's Porch.

You might be wondering why that was its name, which is a good question. Basically, I had learned from past experience to ask God what He wanted to name the various churches, even though my own thought was to call this new church The Lord's Gathering. I just loved the idea that God's sons and daughters could gather together and hang out with one another and with the Lord.

I knew it was important to ask the Lord what He thought about the name, however, and so I did. There was no hesitation. He said "No, I don't want you to name it the Lord's Gathering." For a week, I tried to convince the Lord that it was a great name and that it captivated my heart for gathering with people, worshipping, and loving Him.

My concept of church had dramatically changed from the first time I walked into one in 1970. What God was doing 46 years ago, however, He is doing differently now. The culture had changed and so the church needed to change. I continued to try and convince God that He should approve the name I had come up with. He told me to google the name, "The Lord's Gathering" so I went and grabbed my computer to look it up.

I soon discovered that there had been a church in Massachusetts named The Lord's Gathering that had lost its way. The Lord asked me, "Do you want to be identified with that?" Obviously, the answer was no, so I then asked Him what His name for the church was. There was no answer; in fact, there was dead silence. It was within a few days that I was reading in the Book of Acts in chapter three that there was a crippled man sitting outside of the Gate of Beautiful begging for money. One day Peter and John saw him and prayed for him. The man was immediately healed, and it says, "They all ran to Solomon's Porch and the people were greatly amazed."

Something just went off inside of me that people would run with joy to go to Solomon's Porch. I knew that Solomon's Porch was part of the temple, and then I recalled the scripture in John 10:23 where is says, "And Jesus walked on Solomon's Porch." Every time in the New Testament where we see that Jesus went to the temple he was going to Solomon's Porch. There Jesus would preach, teach, and confront the Pharisees and Sadducees. It was also the place where the apostles would preach and teach, the birth place of the New Testament church.

I researched its history and discovered that when Nebuchadnezzar destroyed the original Temple he didn't destroy Solomon's Porch because of its beauty and splendor. When Herod rebuilt the temple, he incorporated into the rebuilding the Temple around Solomon's Porch. Then I read Acts 5:12-16, *"And through the hands of the apostles many signs and wonders were done among the people. And they were all with one accord in Solomon's Porch. Yet none of the rest dared join them, but the people esteemed them highly. And believers were increasingly added to the Lord, multitudes of both men and women, so that they brought the sick out into the streets and laid them on beds and couches, that at least the shadow of Peter passing by might fall on some of them. Also, a multitude gathered from the surrounding cities to Jerusalem, bringing sick people and those who were tormented by unclean spirits, and they were all healed."*

God Does Things as He Wills

How did "The Porch" start? It was sometime in late February 2009 that we made the official transfer of Jericho into the hands of another pastor. I had gone on a medical sabbatical in August of 2008, and immediately there was a movement to replace me and to take the church in a new direction. I was hurt and confused and didn't know what to do, but one thing I was certain of -- I needed to continue to serve God. Before my sabbatical I was having a desire birthed in me to move into more of an apostolic/prophetic ministry and to travel more. Starting in 1995 I traveled to Haiti on numerous occasions and sent a number of teams there to work with Pastor Carlo. I was growing weary of being a senior pastor.

It was somewhere in March 2009 after transferring the church that a couple I was very close to called and asked me to come over that Sunday. That day when we pulled into Rick and MC's driveway, there were a number of cars, and I wondered to myself what was going on. Walking in the house, I saw about 40 people in the living room, which was set up like a cell group. There was a table full of food that seemed obvious we would have at some point later. A keyboard was set up for worship, which we had and which was incredible. The presence of God was so tangible, so loving, so kind, so healing. After worship, the people there turned to me and asked me if I had something to share. I usually do, and that particular morning I shared briefly. It was so therapeutic! God was already healing me of all the recent events.

For the next ten months we met every Sunday, and this home became our sanctuary. People would call and say, "We want to come to your church." We'd tell them no because we had no room and I didn't want to pastor. I didn't want to deal with problems. I didn't want to do counseling.

Then that December the Lord spoke to me that it was time to have a public ministry again. I asked the Lord where he wanted me to go. His response was very surprising. He said, "Brian, you can go anywhere you want to go." He was able to say that because he knew that I would go where there was a need. Almost immediately I began to hear the cry of the city of Fall River that I had heard earlier in 1995. I felt the Holy Spirit tell me that I had unfinished business there.

I then began the search for a place for us to gather. I eventually called a realtor who knew of a place on North Main Street which was a ready-to-move-in location. We had a sanctuary, my office which would serve as a classroom, and a room for a nursery. We had our first service on Christmas Eve 2009, and we all know there's something special about Christmas Eve.

Another Cloud Fills the Church

The first was in 1996 at Jericho when we moved into a new 10,000 square foot building on Christmas Eve. There was Christmas Eve 2015 when I had left and was driving home and Pastor Tom called me to come back. When I got inside the building he had me come and stand on the altar area and look up. What did I see but another cloud filling the cathedral ceiling of this old Episcopal Church we were renting. It was unlike the cloud in my hotel room and unlike the cloud I saw at Jericho. This cloud was more like a mist or a fog. Perhaps in this we can see God moving, but differently than He had in the past.

It was the week before Christmas, and as I was in service worshipping I felt the Lord tell me that it was time to transfer/recognize Pastor Tom Mello as the Senior Pastor of Solomon's Porch. He had been doing the job for more than a year. Over the last number of years, I had been traveling a lot. I was away over 12 weeks in 2016 and am already scheduled to be away more in 2017. On Sunday morning January 15th, I was praying and asking the Lord if He was sure He wanted me to release the church or whether He wanted me to wait.

Within a few minutes the chair I was sitting on began to shake. It shook so much that I went home and googled earthquakes. The floor and my chair shook for over five minutes. I got up and asked Pastor Steve sitting one chair from me if he felt anything. He affirms he did but when I asked other people that day if they had felt anything they all said, "No." To me it was God shaking things up and saying, "Yes, make Pastor Tom the senior pastor."

Letting Go

It was the following week on January 22, 2017 when we made the official announcement that Pastor Tom and his wife Lisa would be installed as the new senior pastors on Sunday, March 18.

One of my recent thoughts of the day was called "Letting go," which is all about needing to release various aspects of our lives before God opens new doors. It's become clear that it's time to let go and to step out in faith, and since this decision has been made, I've received three phone calls asking me to new places.

It's been three years since the Lord gave me the scripture from Isaiah 43:19 saying, *"Behold, I will do a new thing, Now it shall spring forth; Shall you not know it? I will even make a road in the wilderness and rivers in the desert."* But in order for Him to do that, I had to embrace and apply verse 18, *"Do not remember the former things, nor consider the things of old."*

When the Porch started I knew that God wanted a new model. He wanted a new type of church, and I had no idea what that looked like. Even as I'm writing this book, God is still defining what that looks like. Everything that I've ever done has always grown quickly and exponentially… except… this church plant. Why? It's because if we grew too quickly and exponentially we would repeat the patterns and models of what I've done for 40 years. God had to take the old out of me and still does so that I can perceive the new.

Gratefully, though, we have this amazing core of people who have been willing to go through this process of learning to do "new."

The new for us was not to have church as usual. It was and is about His showing us what to do and our willingness to wait for Him to show us and for Him to send the right people. You would think, for example, that a church would have a Sunday school program? Well, that is important to have, but unless God sends the right people we don't do it "just because." We have had people who were willing to do Sunday school but who didn't have the anointing or the "breath" to do it. We refused to have a Sunday school just for the sake of having one. Unless God supplies the right person with the right anointing we don't go ahead. Certainly, we felt the pressure to have one, but pressure is not presence. Waiting for God to move avoids the birthing of Ishmaels.

Being Led

Being led by the Holy Spirit means that we seek to discern what God is doing or *wants* to do rather than living by what God *used* to do. Much like the sons of Issachar, we need to discern the times (1 Chronicles 12:32). It requires putting away agendas and old ideas and being willing to wait, which can be a monster. If we are busy being busy, even with doing good things, it will be almost impossible to see what God is doing or wants to do. We are often too busy walking in the natural that we aren't able to walk in the supernatural.

Solomon's Porch is different from any church that I have been in or even known about. God has been and is working differently here than in all my years previously. New means new, not remodeled. There are many things we would like God to do, but we're learning to rejoice in what He is doing now. We can be so focused on our desires that we miss the present, which tends to cause us great discontent. In Exodus 33:14 there was a two-fold promise given to Moses that we too need to embrace. It was first, that they would have God's presence, and second, that God would give them rest.

Jesus said in John 8:29: *"I always do those things that please Him."* Why don't we follow this example?

God and the Homeless Shelter

Four years ago, we became involved in the Fall River Overflow Homeless Shelter program. In the first year, we began by just helping out but by the second year had completely taken it over. From January second through March tenth we oversee a shelter which houses up to 22 people a night.

Being involved in the overflow shelter has given us favor and recognition with the city of Fall River. The mayor and Department of Community Services have reached out to us not only for the overflow shelter but to operate a warming center in the Government Center (City Hall) during severe weather. Our little community is having a direct impact on the city. I would say that is a miracle.

It has been eight years since God started Solomon's Porch. It has been a time of learning and unlearning. It has been about finding contentment in what God is doing instead of being discouraged about what He's not, also about learning to rest and live in His presence. Jesus promised us rest. We were created to be a people of rest. Man was created on the sixth day, and his first day on earth was the day of rest.

I would say that we are and have been watching the Holy Spirit move. It has been a struggle but is still rewarding. The exciting thing is that God has used this time and continues to use it to position us for our corporate and individual future. The prophet in 2 Chronicles 20 told Jehoshaphat and Israel to *"position yourself."* In 2 Kings 9 Elisha says to the young prophet, *"Get yourself ready."* I believe that we have been in a time of preparation where God has been moving in multiple ways.

Apostolic and Prophetic –
Here, There, and Everywhere

In this chapter, I'll share some of my apostolic, prophetic travels. Perhaps one of the first questions you might be asking is at what point I knew I was called to travel. The answer is, the very day I was saved.

I recall kneeling on the tile floor and giving my life to the Lord in the spring of 1970, and one of the things I was shocked to hear from the Holy Spirit was Revelation 11. I grabbed my Bible and proceeded to read about the two witnesses and heard God say, "That's you and not you."

I knew exactly what He was saying. I knew God was using the two witnesses as a type and shadow. I knew also that the two witnesses were "Jews" and though I wasn't one of them, I was to travel and be a witness of God's transforming power.

Even as I write this I am overwhelmed that God would say such things to me and that I somehow didn't go off into some weird, tangential thinking that I was the world's next spiritual superstar.

I do have to admit that for many years leading up to my travel, I was wondering why the season hadn't yet started.

The answer was really quite simple – I wasn't ready. I wasn't mature enough. My prophetic gift had to grow, and perhaps more importantly I needed to grow as a person. I needed to learn when to speak and when not to. I hadn't yet realized that the people to whom I would speak and minister, Jesus had died for. I hadn't yet realized that people were the most precious things to God's heart, so I needed to love and honor them above all else. I was too full of myself.

And while I am not saying that I've fully arrived, by His grace I continue to grow.

If God is calling you, He will be faithful to equip and train you for what He is calling you to do. While I know that people now typically have a shorter training period, I do not regret for a moment how He has mentored me. My first real prophetic/apostolic journey was in 1995 when I traveled to Haiti. That was a full twenty-five years after I had become a believer.

God Was in India

Over the past ten years I've witnessed many miraculous things God has done as I've traveled both nationally and internationally. Perhaps a good place to start is with my trip to India in 2006.

Our team was busy from early in the morning to late at night. We started with prayer in the chapel at 6:00 a.m., had breakfast, and then returned to chapel. After that the women went off to the Christian school and Al and I went off to teach in their seminary. Following that we went back to chapel, had lunch, an afternoon break, dinner, and then returned to chapel for outreach. That was a normal day.

Every night the small chapel was full of people, many having walked for miles to come to a service. There are three particular services I am compelled to share.

It was in the middle of the week when Pastor Matthew was invited to a small village about 35 minutes from his compound. When we arrived, beautiful leis were placed on all of us – a custom to honor guests. It was my understanding that the village's population was about 120 people, and of those, there were only two Christians. We were sitting there when the pastor came over to me and asked me to get up and preach. I asked him why they wanted to listen to me when they had 330,000,000 gods. Yet I understood that if I could demonstrate the Kingdom of God, I could perhaps gain their attention.

I walked out and stood among the women and children. The men do not sit with them; they sit by themselves. I started praying for the women, and every single one of them collapsed under the power of God and fell to the ground. The men, seeing this happening, rushed into the middle of all the women and children, and began to insist we pray for them first. While this is the Indian culture, it's not the Kingdom-of-God culture.

I asked our team to hold back the men so I could continue to pray first for a woman, then a child, and then a man. Everyone I prayed with fell to the ground and was there for a while. The first man I prayed for was drunk. When I laid hands on him he hit the ground like he was shot from a cannon and was there for at least 30 minutes. When he got up, his breath smelled like lilies, and he was stone sober.

At one point, I stopped and looked down and the ground was littered with men, women, and children. It really wasn't dirt they were on either; it was dung, which the Indians would roll out to dry in order to prevent the dirt from turning to mud.

Before I knew it was dusk, and I was still praying for people. A man came to me and said that he wasn't a Christian but that he would be honored if we would come to his house to continue ministering to people. It was the strangest thing: he had a light outside of his home. It was the only light in the village, and I didn't hear a generator running. To this day I don't know how that light was on.

We walked to his house. I had a man on both of my arms navigating me in the dark. They walked me right through an open sewer which caused my shoes and the cuffs of my pants to get wet. When we arrived at his home, the girls on the team took the people who had been touched by God and taught them the simple Christian songs; most of the time they just sang "Hallelujah." By the time I finished praying for people it was very dark, and the pastor said to me, "You need to preach now." I had no idea what to preach. I was so overwhelmed myself with the power of God that it was ridiculous. At that point in time in my mind I heard, "Preach the Christmas story," and that's what I did. I taught about how a Savior was born to save people from their sins.

Then it came time to make an altar call. What happened next was miraculous, as 70-75 people were willing to commit their lives to Christ. In this culture, such a commitment means that they are considered dead to their families.

The following night we drove 30 minutes to another location. We arrived at an incomplete small block building serving as a church for the area. As they were setting up the chairs and the generator I noticed a woman standing near me who did not look well. I took from her the baby she was holding and gave the child to Caren, who was our missions director. I turned and prayed for the woman right there outside the small chapel. She collapsed under the power of God.

Before I knew it, there had to be 30 people lying in the dirt who had come for prayer. One of the remarkable things is that they had never seen people fall down under the power of God, so it wasn't the power of suggestion. As they lay on the ground, dogs and chickens would walk between them. You had to see to it to believe it. They finally set up the lights and chairs, and the generator was running.

We had gone there to dedicate the building. Dedicating a building is a very big event in a community. It is so important that the president (mayor) of that village and his cabinet members are there. Again, they placed a beautiful floral lei on each of our necks. The pastor came and said, "It's time for you to preach." My response was the same as the night before. Why would they want to listen to me when they have 330,000,000 gods?

I got out of my seat and walked over to the president and his cabinet members, and they all fell under the power of God. I do not know how long I prayed, but I believe that I prayed for nearly everyone, and if not, it was definitely close. Everyone was touched by the power of God. I made an invitation for people to accept Christ after I shared, and there were so many who accepted.

The third incredible thing I witnessed was on Friday night in the chapel of the compound where we had been staying, and we saw God move powerfully among the people who had come. Some had walked for hours, and the place was filled beyond capacity. The power of God filled the night air. People were delivered from demons, gave their hearts to Christ, were healed, and many fell under the power of God.

The next morning, we were going to have a special service to baptize eight people, but the number rose to over 25. In the morning when I awoke, I was told that 150 people never left the chapel. They stayed all night because they wanted to be in God's presence to see what He would do.

I taught a brief class about the meaning of baptism. After the class, we began the service and then it was time to baptize people. The pastor asked me to lay hands on people before they walked down the fifteen steps to enter the baptismal under the floor. I tried to talk the pastor out of it and said that it would be better to pray for them afterwards, but he said no. I did as I was asked, and every person I prayed for fell under the power of God and stayed down for a long period of time. When they got up they needed help maneuvering down the stairs.

Every day we saw God move. Every day people were saved, healed, and touched by the power of God. Late one morning as we were coming out of chapel before lunch, three men came into the chapel. They told me that they had walked four hours to get there and came because they heard God was there. I turned to the first man and said, "You are a pastor," to the next man, "I said you are not a pastor," and to the third, "I said you are a pastor." It was true. I laid hands on them and after waiting over 30 minutes for them to get up, which they never did, I left and had lunch.

The following is the testimony I received from the pastor who translated for me 11 years ago. I don't use his name for safety reasons. He says,

My memories are I saw a great move of the Holy Spirit in India. Many people fall down in Spirit. Many Demon spirits has left. Many, many miracles happened. Many accepted Christ as their savior. In that meetings God spoke to me to go to the poor people but for some more years I disagreed to the Spirit of God. Finally God brought me to the place. You prophesied to me about this from Isaiah 61.

An E-mail from Pastor Joseph: October 2012:
After Return from Romania

Shalom Pastor Brian,

How are you?

How was the trip back to your home?

To God be the glory for everything He has done in these 12 days through you, Pastor Brian!

Your visit to Romania was prophetical, providential and magnificent. It was at the appointed time!

The Presence of God could be felt within moments after the school on prophecy started here in Brasov. Then, we traveled several hours to Hateg where I sat and watched God use you prophetically. The next day we once again drove several hours to a national pastor's conference in Cluj.

At this conference God has touched many hearts of pastors and opened very many doors of collaboration in the future for the great spiritual awakening in Romania. Everything was in its season! There were divine meetings, divine connections, and divine messages for people.

Truly, the Holy Spirit started many fires in Romania by you. The miracle is that this fire has been touched so many interdenominational people, people from many churches, such as: Pentecostal, Baptist, Plymouth Brethren, Seventh Day Adventist, Orthodox Churches and many other churches across denominational lines.

We are so grateful to God for you, and we would say a big thank you to your wife and to the church who understood God's time for allowing you be full part of what God is doing in our country.

Thank you for accepting a position on our pastoral team. and for accepting our invitation to have you mentor us.

I am looking forward for you to come back at the end of February 2013 for the national conference with the all the churches in our Federation, which takes place in Oradea and then to visit other key churches that we may develop a strategic plan to impact all of Romania.

With much consideration,

In His ministry for Life,

Pastor Joseph Belea,

Rebirth Church, Brasov – Romania

A Thank You for Ministering in the Village of Caransebes From Pastor Marian Zamfir

I want to give a feedback of your coming here. You were a blessing to us. You left blessings, encouragement, renewal.

The people saw how the prophetic gift works, and they were happy to receive your message and your anointing. We will rejoice when will you will come again, we are waiting for you. My house and family is blessed through you.

My pastor friends from Severin, he was with us in Caransebes for the meetings and from Iasi wants to go to them too. They are expecting you and so do we.

Greetings to your wife and kids. God bless you and your family, and straighten you in your work.

Thank you again for being a part of what God is doing in Romania.

Haiti

I started going to Haiti in 1995. On the first trip, I remember the stench as we disembarked the plane and also recall seeing the 50 or so children whose parents had broken their legs and arms and never had them set, the purpose to engender sympathy and spare change.

We drove nine hours to the first church Pastor Carlo oversees. It was a "building" comprised of thatched walls made of palm branches outfitted with wooden benches. Carlo asked us if we wanted to see his other church. We said "Sure." What he didn't tell us was that the journey to get there involved traveling through rice fields filled with dung, up a mountain, down a mountain, then up another mountain.

Besides that, it was 104 degrees and very humid. We reached the top of the mountain, and no one was around. We went inside the church, and I laid down on a bench because at this point I didn't feel well. The people started arriving in their pressed white dresses and shirts. They wouldn't come into the church unless they dressed well to honor God. They were singing, and I was lying on the bench when I suddenly felt like I was hooked up to an IV. Within a couple minutes I was totally restored.

We headed down the two mountains, and I changed into my bathing suit to baptize people in the river. There is a story here, but I'll just say that a donkey was 50 feet from me, and his bathroom results were heading my way! There was a blind woman who had walked down the mountain largely on her own in order to be baptized. I prayed for people after they were baptized, and they were slain in the Spirit and lay floating in the water. I have seen this at every baptism I do. It is similar to the baptism of Jesus where in Matthew 3:16-17 it says, "When He had been baptized, Jesus came up immediately from the water; and behold, the heavens were opened to Him, and He saw the Spirit of God descending like a dove and alighting upon Him. And suddenly a voice came from heaven, saying, 'This is My beloved Son, in whom I am well pleased.'" This is common to all our baptisms.

Everything was awesome until this woman stepped into the water. Then...the twilight zone. The wind started blowing strongly, and instantly there was heavy rain. It was like someone threw a switch. Oh, and the woman was screaming. I told the demon to stop and get out. The woman collapsed and the freak weather ended immediately.

It was still 103 degrees at 8:30 p.m. We ate, went to bed lying on hay bales, and watched a three-foot lizard run around the ceiling as the voodoo drums started. I have never heard such hair-raising screams in all my life. I was thinking, "My first trip to Haiti, and I am going to get killed!"

It was so hot. I remember the voodoo drums stopping at 3:30 a.m. and finally being able to sleep. We got up and during breakfast I prophesied to the pastor the same thing that Pastor Carlo had said to him through most of the night before.

I remember going to Balix and me preaching and Carlo interpreting. I would say something, and Carlo would say nothing. I asked Carlo, "Are you going to say that?" He replied, "I have already said it." For the 21 years since I have traveled to Haiti, this has been happening. Pastor Carlo very often knows what I am going to say before I say it. Talk about being one!

That morning people were prophesied to and delivered. I prophesied to the pastor of Balix that he didn't like the people and that he was stealing money from the tithe. The people were shocked and looking at one another because they knew this was true. Pastor Carlo then asked him to verify this, and he did. He was asked if he wanted to repent, and he said, "No." Carlo ended up paying him what he was owed as a salary even though he had stolen money, as he didn't want him going around saying that he had been cheated.

There were numerous pastor conferences where I told the pastors who they were, their personality, and their giftings -- the same way Jesus speaks to Peter and Nathaniel in John one and the woman at the well in John chapter four. Year after year God continues to speak to His people.

December 2012 Haiti

In December of 2012 I was able to take Pastors Tom Mello and Rob Silvia to Haiti. It was a trip they would never forget, and nothing would have prepared them for it. We got off the plane and walked into a make-shift immigration area where we were then escorted to a special office because we lacked the specifics of where we were staying save for the name of the village. Having Pastor Carlo's phone number in this situation was our saving grace.

Nothing prepares you for being swarmed by airport workers forcefully trying to carry your luggage and refusing to take no for an answer. These men were desperate for money, and they walked with us all the way to where Pastor Carlo picked us up. For a first-time traveler, that was frightening.

Once you leave the airport the first thing you become aware of is the stench. It can honestly make people nauseous. We arrived at the hotel, and one of the rooms was supposed to be ready, but was a terrible mess. Someone had had a party there, and it was bad. We were notified by the hotel that the room was ready. Upon arriving we discovered that while the room was picked up, the sheets hadn't been changed. Welcome to Haiti.

The next day we piled into a Toyota 4x4, and I mean piled. Pastor Carlo was bringing supplies, and he had picked up a number of pastors and other men who would eventually carry all our luggage and other items. We drove four hours, maybe longer and finally stopped. We were thinking that the church was just a short way from where we parked the truck. Well, that was not the case.

We headed down a muddy path for quite some time, and thank God Pastor Carlo had brought men with him, because they carried everything. I forgot how long we walked somewhere, perhaps 45 minutes, and then we saw it. It was a river. Okay, we thought, how in the world are we going to cross? The answer: hollowed-out trees that they'd made into canoes. We just had to laugh.

On the way over Pastor Tom led the young man paddling the boat to Christ. We arrived on the other side and had to hike even further to the church compound, where we were shown our accommodations. Pastors Tom and Rob were in one room, and I was in another. Rob had an old army cot, and Tom and I had mattresses on the concrete floor.

At night Pastor Tom put deet around his mattress to prevent thousands of tiny insects from crawling onto it. The outhouse was beyond filthy, as there was a hole but not everyone hit it. The shower was equally bad. The food? Well, welcome to Haiti.

We had gone there to do a pastors' conference. I remember that during one of the services two pastors were fighting over the microphone, because they both wanted to lead worship. Worship was very loud, and truth be told, it sounded exactly like the voodoo worship we heard at night off in the distance. The difference was in the words. After we observed this we were determined to introduce more intimate worship. It was a powerful time, and God moved and transformed many lives.

Here is an email I received from Pastor Carlo shortly after we returned. He wrote:

You have been used by God to help the Haitian leaders to put their community upside down. The first feedback I got was from Balix where people said as they started worshipping God in a new way it was for the first time in their life, and the church was so filled with the presence of God.

Pastor Noel reported to Tom Brumbley that some angels came to Etang Arnoux (the name of the village we stayed in), and many lives have been changed and many great decisions have been taken.

Other Leaders reported that now they have a better vision on the BAPTISM in the HOLY SPIRIT.

I hope someday that you can come back to help us by the grace of God to push the wall of darkness in Haiti and to open leaders' eyes on what God really wants and expects from them.

Thanks again for honoring our invitations and thanks also for being so patient with us as; we know it cost you a lot to be with us. It was a total commitment (when I asked Carlo what he meant he said – he means walking in love, humility, honor of others, genuinely caring for people, not walking in high regard on oneself in pride, true sincerity – very humbling.) The commitment of the first and the biggest lesson we learned from your team according to the testimony of many of us. I urge you my brother to keep on HUMBLE YOURSELF to keep on TEACHING BY EXAMPLE our God will always glorify through your life.

Youth Retreats and Meetings

I have done numerous youth meetings and retreats throughout the years. For the majority, prior to the meeting they had never seen the power of God touch lives. I've ministered in evangelical churches, charismatic churches, Dutch Reform churches, the list goes on.

I am continually awestruck by what I see God do to young people who have never seen someone fall under the power of God.

Then…it happens to them. To see young people on the floor weeping and hugging one another. Many too are told about their life calling. It is so difficult to express the joy that fills the room.

I remember one night the two pastors came to sit in the meeting. They wanted to see if what was happening was genuine. They sat in the back of the room and over the course of the next four hours could not believe what they saw and heard. One of the pastor's sons along with another young man came for prayer, and both laid on the floor for over an hour under the power of God. When they awoke, separately from one another they expressed an identical vision they'd had. When they spoke to one another, it was incredible to hear them compare what they'd both seen. There was such joy in that room.

One young man couldn't get up for hours, and it was decided that he should spend the night lying on the church floor. This is because they were concerned that when he woke up he'd want to drive home, and it's common that people touched by the power of God find themselves unable to drive.

When we were ready to leave, we were able to sit him up though his legs were stiff, and he was unable to walk unassisted. We helped him to his car, and his brother drove him home.

One of the results of our youth meetings is that the youth arrive early for church on Sunday and with hearts on fire are eager to join the intercessors in interceding for the church. This doesn't happen just one Sunday but goes on for several weeks. One meeting in the Episcopal Church brought the youth leader forward for prayer. She fell under the power of God, and her mother came running to kneel beside her.

This same night a young minister and his wife came to the meeting. Before it began we had had dinner with them, during which I said, "You're pregnant." They were stunned because no one knew; she had just learned she was pregnant. The following are remarks from Father Slade about our time together.

October 13, 2013 – Youth Meeting in Coxsackie, New York

The move of God in New York: *"For I will pour water on him who is thirsty, And floods on the dry ground." Isaiah 44:3*

This was the word The Holy Spirit gave Friday night to a room full of young adults (which we often identify as teens). The night was utterly amazing. You had to be there to begin to comprehend God's affection for these young people. He spoke to them on vision and making all their decisions through it. He also spoke about how unforgiveness would hinder them living out of their vision.

Then it happened that God fulfilled His word, *"I will pour water on him who is thirsty, and floods on the dry ground."* Young people hungry and thirsty for God to touch and change their lives came for prayer. It is always such an amazing and wondrous thing to watch the Holy Spirit radically touch and change lives. While praying for these young people there were perhaps six who were on the floor for two hours. The reason I know it was two was that one of their friends actually timed how long they were down. Of the six, four of them told us they couldn't move. One young person laid there with his eyes open able to talk but unable to move a muscle. As he lay there he had an experience like Peter did in Acts 10:9-11: *"The next day, as they went on their journey and drew near the city, Peter went up on the housetop to pray, about the sixth hour. Then he became very hungry and wanted to eat; but while they made ready, he fell into a trance and saw heaven opened."*

He saw heaven open, then he saw the cross and the brightness of a white light he had never seen before cover the face of Jesus. He tried to describe colors which he'd also never seen. While in this state the Lord confirmed what he was to do next with his life. We left him alone, allowing God to continue to work on him, when the enemy decided he would try and steal what God had done. We simply said no to the attack and eventually got the young man up and walked him around the room, a very biblical "arise and walk." He needed to exercise/activate faith in what God had done.

A young girl who had never been to one of these meetings came for prayer and two hours later opened her eyes and just lay there smiling. We found out later she was unable to speak or move. God was healing such deep wounds in her from her foster home experience. The second young man lay there for two hours, and when it was time to think about going home, we sat him up but he couldn't speak or move. We found out later that he had had an almost identical experience as the first young man. Heaven opened, and the Holy Spirit told him what he was to do with his life. (A few years later, by the way, he did what God had spoken to him to do.)

The second young lady who had been through a lot of pain that I cannot write about and who had never been in one of these meetings, began to sob and cry uncontrollably. It was obvious the Lord was healing deep wounds. Then after a period of time she wasn't able to be comforted and began coughing. The Lord in His love for her was setting her free. This took some time, but we couldn't interrupt the process. Finally, her foster dad came in, and the Lord spoke to me that she needed the father's love. He came down front and simply held her. Immediately there was an incredible change in her. The process continued, but it was the father's love and not prayer that completed the work.

The meeting started at 7:00 and we left close to midnight. We could have been there much longer, but we needed to get these wonderful young people home. The next morning it was time for church and all of them went to church over an hour before church was to start and there they prayed and interceded for the church. This continued every Sunday for I what I believe was over a year.

God fulfilled Isaiah 44:3 *"For I will pour water on him who is thirsty, And floods on the dry ground."*

Reflections: Wayne and Kerri Flach (Former Youth Leaders)

First Prophetic Word / Personal Experiences

My first time meeting Pastor Brian (PB) was at a small Episcopal church in a small town in upstate New York where PB was asked to come and minister. I had never been in a service prior to this where words of knowledge and prophecies were given to individuals at such a personal level. While worship filled the room the presence of the Lord came and was very strong. While we worshiped PB would interject as he felt led and give personal prophecies. I was slightly nervous because I had never been given a personal word before. PB gave a word to an individual sitting directly behind me and when he finished, walked past me. While I thought I was in the clear, PB quickly turned around and began to speak to me directly about my family, specifically the generations before that had laid an incredibly godly foundation for me. It was a beautiful experience and so personal. What he shared truly was from the Lord and was so encouraging to me and my personal journey.

Since my first experience, my family and I have had the honor of having PB stay with us while he has been in town for different ministry opportunities. I have gotten to know him better and have seen him move with the Holy Spirit. I have also seen the wisdom he uses when ministering that only comes from obedience, growth, and discipline in the Lord.

Youth Events

My wife and I were youth leaders in a small church for a time, and we had the privilege of PB coming and ministering to the teenagers on multiple occasions. After a time of worship, PB would interject as he was led and began to minister to the teens. On each occasion, the services ended with nearly everyone on the floor overcome by the presence of God -- the teens, leaders, and in many cases, parents that had come to pick up their teens. Incredible prophecies were given about life direction, who they were, etcetera. It was so beautiful to see a group of young people surrender themselves before the Father, because when they did, the Father showed up.

Abounding Love /Reflections of Father Tyler Slade

While I have known him for many years, my recent change of churches helped bring an opportunity for me to introduce PB to my pastors. It was not long before my pastors were able to connect and share stories of seeing God work in many ways. PB was given the opportunity to speak and minister at our church on two occasions at this point. He felt led to speak directly to our pastors about coming up to a higher place. The whole congregation witnessed this and was in complete agreement that this was true for some time. Others PB had never met previously were given specific words about how God saw them and what God had for their destinies.

In the next section, we'll look at entries I've shared on Facebook the last three years called "Thought of the Day." Recently a year's worth of these were compiled and published into a book called Musings.

Romania 2013 - 2014

I was reviewing my journal and came across my trip to Romania in late November through early December 2013. I found this entry dated December 1. 2013. To give you a little context, being in Romania in late November and December is like being in New England except it's a little colder. As it's in the mountains, Brasov is colder still. I had written that it had been snowing.

Romania Day 3: 11/22/13

It's just before 7:00 a.m. on Saturday. I tossed and turned most of the night. The hotel won't have coffee until 7:30.

Yesterday was another incredible day. I was up early, did the usual routine, and then packed for Bucharest. Pastor Joseph and I had breakfast then were off to counsel an older man in his 70s. By the time we finished and the Holy Spirit had so graciously stepped into his and his son's lives, they were both excited about attending church on Sunday, and the father even committed to be baptized.

I jumped into his car, we dropped off his wife Emma and their two sons, ran a few errands, and were off to Bucharest. As we were driving there I was under the impression we would arrive, rest, and I then I would minister. You can start laughing now, because about an hour from the city I discovered that when we arrived I would have enough time to brush my teeth and then go to the meeting.

I thought the meeting was for pastors and leaders, yet when I walked in I discovered some pastors, some leaders, and a large number of hungry people. So, guess what? You're right -- what I had prepared was inappropriate for the people present. The speaker ended his session, and it was time for dinner. I passed on dinner and spent the next 45 minutes asking the Lord what in the world He wanted me to say. Honestly it took a while to get over the panic and shock that I was now to minister to a large church facility full of people. I often quote 1 Samuel 10:7 that when the Spirit of God comes upon you *do as the occasion demands because God is with you.*

Sure enough, God was faithful to show me his heart for His people. The service started, and the teacher before me got up to finish his teaching – oh what a train wreck. The hosting pastor then got up and spent about 25 minutes encouraging people to give for the offering. After the offering, I was introduced. As I stepped forward there was no anointing in the room. So, what did I do? As I was told by the Holy Spirit many years ago, "If you don't carry the anointing, stay home."

Thankfully, the Holy Spirit did show up! The night ended up being supernatural as God wove a prophetic fabric that warmed, touched, and overwhelmed all of us. I was led to preach, then stop and prophesy, and then return to preaching. This was the pattern for one and a half hours. Pastor Joseph interpreted, and wow, what a flow of the Spirit. I was in awe as the Holy Spirit touched lives in such a profound way.

We were supposed to leave this morning but they asked if I could come back just in case the Holy Spirit wanted to do more. So off to spend time asking the question, "Holy Spirit, what do you want to do?"

The following entry rejoices over all the doors God opened for me to bring the Message of the Kingdom of God.

Romania Day 12 - 12/1/13

It is 9:05 p.m., and I just returned from a joint service with several churches where I had the honor of bringing the short but meaningful word of the Lord. It was during dinner that Pastor Joseph began sharing and told me to look at all the doors God had opened for me in just a few years. Here are the doors God opened:

I spoke in front of all the traditional evangelical churches and the Mayor.

I spoke twice at the Pastors Federation of new churches.

I spoke twice at the Watcher's movement

I spoke a prophetic word to the new leaders of the next generation

Tonight, I spoke to many, many Pentecostal and charismatic churches.

All this has happened in the last two years. Amazing!

This morning I was up early and out the door by nine to drive to the mountains for an outside baptism. Yes, I said outside. I arrived, and when worship was almost over Pastor Joseph turned to me and said, "You are up next." Well, this was a surprise, because we had never discussed my speaking. Because it was a baptism service, I assumed that he would want to speak.

The verse *"be ready in season and out of season"* comes to mind. As with any baptism, the people being baptized invite family and friends to come and share in this very important moment in their lives. For many people visiting, the concept of baptism by immersion is outside of their experience/knowledge base. Most of them are familiar with being sprinkled with water as an infant. It would be highly unusual that any of those people who had been invited had ever seen a minister do prophetic ministry.

With that in mind I knew many of them would be highly skeptical of people receiving prophetic words. The normal reaction is that the words being spoken are not true or are facts that the person speaking already knows about the person. I heard the Lord say, "Demonstrate that prophetic ministry is real." I know the Lord spoke this to me in order to give creditability to the prophetic words that would be spoken over people's lives. As I ministered about the meaning of baptism, I would stop my teaching and then approach a number of people who were visiting and give them prophetic words. As the Lord began to tell them about their lives and circumstances, they were shocked. A few of them asked how I knew those things and then went on to say that I was right. When the Holy Spirit was finished, they believed in the power of God manifested through prophetic ministry. What a joy it is to introduce people to the gifts of the Spirit!

With snow all around us the air was very brisk, so they poured hot water into a large, plastic pool. Just before we entered the pool they gave me and Pastor Joseph clergy robes to wear. Yes, become all things to all men.

Pastor Joseph and I baptized 15 people. One of the young women we baptized was the blind girl that God had healed on my last trip there. As people were baptized heaven opened as it did at Jesus' baptism, and I prophesied over each one. Remember that the Father prophesied over Jesus at his baptism. The baptism was filled with the presence of God. There was such joy there that everyone, even the former skeptics, remarked how they could feel it. This was another supernatural experience which changed many lives.

Romania Day 9: 11/7/14

Here we are in Oradea. It was supposed to be a three-hour ride from Balomir, yet it turned out to be five and a half. We are about 25 miles from the Hungary border.

We arrived late for the time I was supposed to minister. The man who took my place made his point several times, which was difficult to hear over and over. The Romanians see themselves as full of shame and guilt and have little or no understanding of sonship.

The organizer of the conference is one of the most influential men in the Pentecostal and Charismatic movements. He was so happy to see me. He asked me to minister for an hour and then two hours tomorrow.

It was a definite challenge following someone who continued to point out over and over what the people needed to do. Thank God for the anointing.

I probably haven't done a very good job telling you how we are turning upside down the church culture of Romania--not only their culture, but their theology and the way they worship. God has so honored the message and method of what we are saying by the incredible anointing of His presence.

When I say they have never seen the worship Troy and Paula are doing, I do mean they have never seen it. People sit overwhelmed and full of joy and peace, not wanting the meetings to end. They just want to sit and be with God.

Though we have two hours tomorrow I just went for it today, not mincing any words concerning what might offend them. I told them that music there, and also in America, was full of noise which hinders our ability to hear God. After this, very appropriately Troy and Paula sang, and the presence of God filled the room. We have started a revolution. People just sat and enjoyed God loving them. I ministered to the organizer and one of his leaders. The Holy Spirit spoke to the worship leader and another woman, all within the hour they gave us. The people couldn't believe an hour had gone by.

We hadn't eaten since ten so we were hungry. We ate and came back to the hotel where Wi-Fi is only available in the lobby. Our bedroom… well, I am considering not taking a shower.

It's now 9:45, and I am in the lobby sitting on a sofa with no padding on the seat. We pack our luggage and car for 8:30, have breakfast, minster from 10:00 to 12:00, and jump in the car for a seven-hour ride back to Brasov.

Tomorrow will be a big day, as we continue to reshape the culture here. We have been blessed to have Pastor Joseph interpret for me. Having a well-known pastor with great credibility has given us the open door and trust we've needed. We are doing prophetic ministry and prophetic worship in churches, and it is completely new to them. Here at the conference it is a radical new way.

All of us so appreciate your prayers, and to those who so graciously sacrificed financially, know that you are having a part in bringing revival to Romania.

December 31, 2014: Thought of the Day: God Went to a Funeral Mass Yesterday

Yesterday I spent a good part of my day supporting a close friend of nearly 30 years. His mother died on Christmas Eve, and yesterday I attended her funeral mass. There are a couple of things I wish to share about it. (Actually, after writing I will hold the second thought for another day.)

Let me begin by saying that the Holy Spirit was at the funeral mass. I am a former Catholic "basher," but the Holy Spirit dealt with that in the late seventies. The scripture says, "Wherever two or three are gathered IN MY NAME, I WILL BE THERE." If

God's presence depended on correct theology, He would never show up.

As we entered the church there was a young lady singing, "Be not afraid, I go before you always." This song has to be close to 40 years old. I am telling you that the presence of God fell on me, and my eyes began to puddle, the voice of God repeating, "BE NOT AFRAID; I GO BEFORE YOU ALWAYS." Can you hear that this morning? I can hear His voice so clearly in that. In fact, this would be a good place to stop and "muse" to see what the Holy Spirit wants to say to us about those eight words. The next part of the song says, "Come follow me and I will give you rest." Can you hear His voice? Hasn't God been speaking about rest? Is it that we will find rest the more we follow him?

So here I am sitting in a funeral mass and God is present and clearly speaking. The mass continued and another song was sung. I felt compelled to raise both of my hands in worship. Indeed, if we are open to the working of the Holy Spirit, He will show up in the most unusual places. Yes, he is omnipresent! One of the deacons got up to do a reading and read from Revelations 21:1-8. If you have a chance, take a peek at it. It is so full of hope. The beginning of verse 3 says, *"And I heard a loud voice from heaven saying,"* and at that moment it was if God's voice began to thunder as the deacon continued, *"Behold, the tabernacle of God is with men, and He will dwell with them, and they shall be His people. God Himself will be with them and be their God."* I heard the Spirit say, "I am coming soon to be among you and my people will be used in unique and powerful ways." Then verse five was read, and it so confirmed what God has been speaking about "doing a new thing." Revelations 3:5: *"Then He who sat on the throne said, Behold, I make all things new."* And He said to me, "Write, for these words are true and faithful." God is saying, "Write it down; I am not a liar; I am about to do something new. Write it down. I will do it!"

I was sitting drinking in all that God was doing, and then He told me that on Sunday morning what he wants me to share is about the need for a new wine skin so he can pour in new wine. If that wasn't enough, when the priest took the incense near the end of the service and was waving it toward the people sitting in the pews, I was hit in my chest as if a soft lighting bolt had struck me. I'm not kidding! When it hit me, I was actually pushed backwards in the pew. The presence of God was so overwhelming, and there was such peace, joy, and also a sense of hope. I had just been touched by God.

Yes, at a Catholic funeral mass God was present. My life is richer because of yesterday. My life was changed because of yesterday. Our God is among us and he is doing great things. Are we open to hear and receive from God in places we might not expect?

Remember Naaman? He limited how God could speak because of his preconceived ideas of how He was going to move. Part of the new is just that. That God will speak and move outside of our past experiences. That He is moving and will continue to move outside of our current mind set. I believe we are going to be shocked at how God is going to shatter our little paradigms.

God went to a funeral mass yesterday!

God Moves in a Coffee House:
An Ordinary Night Becomes Supernatural

Last night I was in a coffee house in East Bridgewater, MA, and as I sat watching people come in, I had no idea what God's intentions were. A coffee house is typically where music is shared and people come from different churches, often people who have not committed to Christ. That is exactly the group that gathered, but this was no normal coffee house. There was barely a seat available. From what I was told this was very unusual. People had no idea what to expect, but they were told that something supernatural would occur. Turns out they weren't prepared for what was going to take place.

After a time of worship with John Polce I got up and quoted 1 Samuel 10:6 – *"the Spirit of the Lord will come upon you, and you will prophesy with them and be turned into another man."* I stated as I often do that WHEN the Spirit of God comes on us (not IF it comes), that God will empower us to breathe/speak life and WE WILL BE CHANGED INTO ANOTHER MAN. Verse 7: "And let it be, when these signs come to you, that you do as the occasion demands; for God is with you." When the anointing comes on us we should DO AS THE OCCASION DEMANDS. In other words, we need to discern God's heart for the moment rather than arriving with a set agenda.

Imagine that you are standing in a room full of people and you don't know what to do! I told everyone present that while I didn't know what to do, I was asking them to pray that I would be able to capture God's heart for the night. Before I forget, a long-time servant and man who has served me for years showed up to support me with prayer and to stand behind people as I prayed for them. It's a good thing he did. Later he told me that on several occasions it took all of his strength not to fall down. (Thanks CF...)

Now what? From this point forward I approached people God highlighted to me. As the Holy Spirit spoke to people they wholeheartedly affirmed that what was spoken was one hundred percent accurate. If that wasn't shocking enough, as I laid hands on people, most of them could not stand up. The majority of the people had never seen or experienced the overwhelming presence of God. As I began to pray for people they would say, "I am not going to fall down." I told them that that was fine; they didn't have to. (I chuckled inside however, because I knew what was coming next.) Sure enough, down they went, God stepping into their lives and beginning to transform them. The Holy Spirit identified gifts, people's pain, and solutions for their problems.

A holy hush encompassed the room as people experienced the presence of God, many for the first time. Several testified that they were healed physically. As I looked across the crowd I noticed something akin to "deer in the headlights" stares, and as the night progressed, a sense of awe and wonder. People were delighting in God and in His presence.

At one point, I felt that the expectation in God was lifting and the performance mentality entered the room. Discerning this, I told everyone what I was sensing and that I would not leave what the Holy Spirit was doing and begin to operate in my gift apart from God's direction and favor. So, I knew that what we all needed at that point was to take our eyes off me and put them back where they should be – on the Lord. After two worship songs, the performance spirit was gone, and God refilled the room with His presence. I prophesied and prayed over a number of people, and the majority of them ended up on the carpet. One woman declared, "I'm not going to fall" (she said this later on as well), yet found herself on the floor, and after a period of time asked, "How did I get here?"

What a joy and honor to see lives changed. I will once again testify of the goodness, the mercy, the compassion, and the transforming power of God.

We were not called to live ordinary lives but extraordinary ones. Today and every day the Holy Spirit will be with us, leading us, guiding us, and teaching us what and what not to do.

Have a supernatural day!

The Holy Spirit Visits a Homeless Shelter

January 14, 2015: Thought of the Day: Writing from Jerusalem

It's 4:00 a.m., and I'm sitting in the overflow homeless shelter. I had to come back tonight to train the 3:00 to 7:00 a.m. team. We are so thankful that so many people have signed up to come and help. If you would like to volunteer you can go to the web and type in fallriveroverflowshelter.com. There is an application you can fill out online.

I can't begin to tell you how rewarding it is to sit and listen to people share their story of how they ended up in the shelter.

Tonight, I was speaking to one man who for multiple years had a serious drug habit. He was living a secret life -- I wonder how many of us have our own -- when one day a family member discovered his secret. The entire family was devastated. As painful as it is to be away from his family, the man is thanking God that he is no longer taking drugs, because for 23 years they were his hidden habit.

Once it was discovered, he turned himself in to get "clean." His first day in the clinic he prayed and asked God to take away his dependence and deep craving for the drug. What did God do but immediately deliver him from any desire whatsoever. As he told me this story, tears ran down his checks.

With his voice quivering he went on to share the pain of not being with his family. Tears flowed like a faucet. As I listened, like so many other volunteers, I simply put my arm around him. After a few minutes he said, "Thank you." I see how every night the people serving here sit, listen, and truly care for people. One man was in another shelter in another town and had heard about this overflow shelter in Fall River, so he had someone bring him here. He told me tonight how wonderful it was to be here, adding that all the volunteers really cared and treated them like real people. He was so thankful that he felt safe and cared for and that by being here it gave him hope. Wow!

In Acts 1:8 it says, *"But you shall receive power when the Holy Spirit has come upon you; and you shall be witnesses to Me in Jerusalem, and in all Judea and Samaria, and to the end of the earth."* We are to be witnesses in our Jerusalem. In the Greek to be a witness means to be one who testifies as in a court of law. Often our witness is not with words but through loving, caring, and listening. What might seem so insignificant can, in fact, change a life. I have written before that I have discovered the power of "Hello," a simple greeting often the key to reaching a person's heart.

You don't have to travel to Africa, Haiti, or some other far-away place to go on a missions trip. Just look around where you live and work and see your Jerusalem.

Writing with joy from Jerusalem!

February 14 - The Holy Spirit is Moving on an Airplane: Day 2 Haiti

I left Boston at 5:15 a.m. and arrived in Miami at 8:45. I jumped on a shuttle train and then walked about 10 minutes to my designated gate. There was Pastor Carlo with a big ear-to-ear grin. We hugged a couple of times and within 25 minutes were boarding a plane for Port Au Prince. I am now in the air. We will arrive in Port Au Prince in a little over two hours and then travel about three hours to Delmas, the central part of Haiti. This will be new for me, as I usually go to the southern part of the country.

I forgot to mention that I prophesied to the woman in Boston who was checking people in for their flights. She stared at me and didn't know how to respond. As we boarded the plane in Miami I had Pastor Carlo sit beside the woman who couldn't speak English. I asked him to give her a word that came to me the moment she sat down.

Earlier February 14: Works of the Holy Spirit: Day 2 Part 2

It is now 9:45 p.m., and I just returned to my room and am looking forward to a shower with no hot water; true, there is none. I was picked up about 6:30, so I had a great afternoon to study, pray, and nap. I am feeling better; thank you for praying.

At dinner tonight I was given the opportunity to prophesy over three more pastors. They all acknowledged the accuracy of the word spoken as well as being delighted in how and in what God spoke to them. On the way to minister to the youth, one of the pastors I had spoken to approached me and said that it was like I had known him his entire life and especially where he is today. It is so awesome that God would speak so clearly to him and to others.

Thus far I have only had a few words for the youth and several for the pastors.

Tonight I reviewed what I had taught them this morning, and at the end of my sharing I asked Pastor Carlo to come and lead them in a commitment prayer. I found out later that he reviewed point by point the things I had shared. In 2 Peter, it says that Peter was reminding them of things he had written in his first letter in order to stir them up and help them remember. Too often we are on to the next truth/nugget before fully grasping the depth of what we've just heard.

We spoke about a need for a vision for our lives. Once we have an understanding of that vision every decision we then make should be through its lens--decisions like who to marry, what jobs to accept, and which jobs to decline. It should encompass our everyday life, what we do and say 24 hours a day. I spoke on being committed to our vision no matter what takes place around us.

I turned the meeting over to Pastor Carlo, and off he went. It was amazing to see and to be a part of. It was necessary to turn the meeting over to him early so that he could speak unhindered by a language barrier. It was a privilege to be in that meeting.

Well, off to the cold shower, then prayer and study time for tomorrow.

Thank you all for praying. pb

Michigan 3/13/15 -- God Shows Up in a Library

It's 7:00 a.m. Friday morning, and I can't wait to tell you what God did last night "in a library." It was just amazing. Truly, the Holy Spirit just loves being in our midst. The Father so wants to manifest Himself. He wants to love on us, encourage us, affirm and confirm who we are, anoint us, and once again remind us that He has personally chosen us to make an impact in this world.

Our meeting started at seven with Britt (Pastor Britt, my nephew) and four young people, the oldest among them maybe 19, and then

Troy. They were used by God to create an atmosphere in which God could dwell and inhabit. Yes, it says, "God inhabits the praises of his people." For about 45 minutes the room was filled with the presence of God. As usual I sat about three quarters of the way back in the room just to be alone and look at the people whom God had brought. For almost the entire time the Holy Spirit didn't show me a thing. I was sitting there praying, and the Holy Spirit was showing me nothing. I was thinking, okay God; we will follow your leading and spend the night in worship.

It was moments later that I received four very brief prophetic words. They were "step forward; don't worry about tomorrow; thank you for all you've done; and you have a prophetic anointing." That was not much to start with considering we had a room full of people. Then He told me to share some verses, the first being Judges 7:15, "And so it was, when Gideon heard the telling of the dream and its interpretation, that he worshiped." The point that the Lord wanted to make is that our response to hearing from God through a dream or in the case of last night, through prophetic words, should be worship. Normally after prophetic meetings I go home into my office and walk around with my hands raised just thanking God for everything he did that night.

Last night when I came back to Tim and Lisa's home where Donna and I are staying, I ate dinner then sat in the living room in the dark thanking Him for an incredible evening. I had done a little more sharing of scripture than I normally do, feeling that I was to speak on our identity as sons and daughters of God. Recently I have been sharing from Ephesians 2:10, *"For we are His workmanship, created in Christ Jesus for good works, which God prepared beforehand that we should walk in them."* The Orthodox Jewish Bible says, "We are his masterpiece." I just love that image!

As is always the case, last night was simply what God accomplished. As I stood to minister those four brief words, God expanded each one. I was and still am in awe of how the Holy Spirit knows us and knows how to reach into all of our lives. Troy did what he always does, which is to take us to a more intimate place of God's presence, with this amazing gift to create new songs as he plays the keyboard. Last night he again sang over a woman prophetically. In Zephaniah it says, *"God rejoices over us with singing."* He had her come sit up front so she could hear what her Father wanted to say to her, which was really powerful!

Along with numerous prophetic words the Lord had shown me, I was to pray for God's impartation into various people's lives. I had certain people come into the main aisle. I then took both of their hands into one of my hands. I didn't lay my hands on their heads, because if God moved on them and they fell to the floor they couldn't say, or those observing couldn't say, that I had pushed them down. As I prayed for people many did fall, but whether a person falls or not is not an indication that God answered one prayer and not another. In fact, some people whose hands I took went onto the floor even before I said a word.

What happened last night? I know this: our lives were changed because God was in the room. As it says in 1 Samuel 10:6: *"when the Spirit of God comes upon us we will be changed into another man."* Simply stated, GOD CAME AND CHANGED OUR LIVES!

Michigan 3/15/15

It's 12:30 a.m. and I am winding down from another extraordinary night where we had the honor of being in the Lord's presence. Again tonight Pastor Britt along with Troy and five very talented and gifted young people brought us to this incredible place of being in the very real and tangible presence of God. It was one of those nights where I was almost too embarrassed to open my mouth and say anything. The room was full of people who just wanted to see God show up and impact their lives. None of us were disappointed.

Once again there was a cross section of young and old. There were a number of young people from a nearby college whom I called "the young prophets." It never ceases to amaze me how God knows each of us so intimately. The Holy Spirit spoke to more than 20 people, and I spent some time mentoring people on how to minister prophetically. I shared what to do and what not do and the danger of feeling the pressure to perform. I shared the need to wait on God and also demonstrated how to wait for the Holy Spirit to show a person what to do next. Troy and I also showed how prophetic music flows harmoniously with prophetic ministry. At times during the night everyone just sat in the presence of God and at other times we all enjoyed laughing at ourselves. I shared how we need to be like Jehoshaphat who said, "I don't know what to do but my eyes are upon you."

At one point, I walked over to Pastor Britt and asked him what he thought God wanted to do. Immediately he approached one of the "young prophets" and talked to him about considering seminary. Well, just recently this young man had begun to ponder this very thing.

In talking to some of the people who attended one or more of the three nights, they all said the same thing; there was nothing like this in the area. They indicated that there was not one church or ministry where they could come and corporately experience both the power and presence of God.

Lord, thank you for allowing us to come. Thank you for the honor to be here.

April 5: Thought of the Day: Easter 2015 and God Among Us!

First of all, happy belated Easter! Here is what took place on the Porch yesterday, where we were honored once again to have God in our midst. I can't begin to describe how utterly amazing it is to have the tangible presence of God in every service. Everyone knows that God is there - everyone.

We are like the women from Matthew 28:9 leaving the tomb whom Jesus greeted by saying, "Rejoice!" They came and held Him by the feet and worshiped Him." Whether we are in church, in our car, or at home, the response to His presence is always worship. It was during worship that I could hear the sound of a large stone being rolled away. According to historical facts they believed the stone was four to six feet in diameter and approximately a foot thick, and depending on the stone used it would weigh between one and two tons.

After worship, I shared that there were many people there who were being kept in their own tombs because they had a stone in front of their hearts. And like the women on the way to the tomb, they were speaking to one another and asking, "Who will roll away the stone from the door of the tomb for us?" (Mark 16:3)

I asked those to stand up who felt trapped by their own stone, one blocking them from experiencing life. At least 50 percent of the church rose to their feet. I declared that God was there to roll the stone away from their hearts. The people who didn't stand then went and prayed for those standing. In the natural it looked like people praying, but in the Spirit stones were being rolled away and people were being liberated from their tombs.

Perhaps this morning you feel trapped and know that a stone is in front of your heart. You can ask the Lord to roll away the stone or call/find someone to pray with you and watch and see what God WILL do.

During our time together the next question I was prompted to ask came from Luke 14:5: *"Why do you seek the living among the dead?"* All too often we are looking in the wrong places for life. We are looking for life among the tombs, in places that represent death. The angels were right when they declared in verse 6: *"He is not here, but is risen!"* We have to stop trying to find life where Jesus is not.

We then read most of 1 Corinthians 15 while stopping to emphasize verses 16-17: *"For if the dead do not rise, then Christ is not risen. And if Christ is not risen, your faith is futile; you are still in your sins!"* Praise God that Jesus rose and is risen and because of this our sins have been taken away. John the Baptist, upon seeing Jesus, declares in John 1:29, *"The next day John saw Jesus coming toward him, and said, "Behold! The Lamb of God who takes away the sin of the world!"*

Jesus takes away sin completely; he doesn't just cover it. He removes not only sin but shame and guilt. Hebrews 9:12-14 says, *"Not with the blood of goats and calves, but with His own blood He entered the Most Holy Place once for all, having obtained eternal redemption. For if the blood of bulls and goats and the ashes of a heifer, sprinkling the unclean, sanctifies for the purifying of the flesh, how much more shall the blood of Christ, who through the eternal Spirit offered Himself without spot to God, cleanse your conscience from dead works to serve the living God?"*

After sharing this I asked if everyone present had asked Jesus to take away their sin and if they had committed their lives to Jesus -- committed <u>not</u> to a church or denomination, but to Jesus. With people's heads bowed we had a number of people commit their life to Jesus. What an incredible day to come from death to life and more somehow on Easter morning. What a day. God was in our midst!

We celebrated communion in a fresh way believing that we would hear testimonies of people being healed physically, spiritually, and emotionally, *"for by his stripes we are healed."* The context of this message comes from Isaiah, Chapter 53, verse 5: *"But He was wounded for our transgressions, He was bruised for our iniquities; The chastisement for our peace was upon Him, And by His stripes we are healed."* and 1 Peter 2:24: *"who Himself bore our sins in His own body on the tree, that we, having died to sins, might live for righteousness—by whose stripes you were healed."*

Easter 2015 and God was among us!

April 17, 2015: Thought of the Day:
The Holy Spirit Goes to Lunch

Yesterday afternoon I met with a man in a Rhode Island restaurant. We had tried to meet twice previously but couldn't manage over the past five or so months to coordinate our schedules.

It was perhaps a year ago that I prophesied to him at La Salette Shrine in Attleboro. He was stunned how the Holy Spirit spoke to him with such clarity. In 1 Corinthians 14:25 it says, that through prophesy, *"the secrets of his heart are revealed."*

I had heard that to his credit he went home and activated the prophetic word he had received. He was facing some real-life critical situations, and the word he had received became the one he would apply in countless situations. So, for one full year he was living by what the Holy Spirit had spoken to him. How wonderful! I so desire others to activate prophetic words like this man, rather than have them sit idle in a person's heart and mind. My friend John would say to me all the time that his friend was activating the word he had received, yet he wouldn't provide any particulars.

So, the three of us decided to meet for lunch. While I had told John that I didn't have anything prophetic for his friend, even so his friend believed that God would speak to him and drove three and half hours to have lunch. Just before I left to go meet with them I prayed and asked the Holy Spirit if He had anything to say to him. He did. First the Spirit wanted him to know "how proud of him" He was that he had clung to and activated the word he had received. Second, He told me that "today marked a day when it was time to move forward with a new prophetic word."

Ten minutes hadn't passed when I told him at least three times he needed to marry the woman he had been dating for a few years. I had no idea that this was something he wanted to do but couldn't because he was waiting for an annulment. While he had filed for it, he was still waiting to receive a notification. John Polce, who talks to his friend every day, just started laughing and shaking his head, adding that the accuracy of what was said was one hundred percent.

While I continued to prophecy, his friend's phone rang three times. Finally, I told him to answer the phone. It was his ex-wife. She had just received a letter from the Church with their decision on the annulment. As we sat there she read the determination for which they had been waiting for two years. The notice read that the annulment had indeed been granted. John and his friend started rejoicing, and I cried. To see God move so quickly, to see Him confirm His word at that moment, is something I will never forget.

Just picture this: you have been waiting two years for a decision regarding your annulment which you've been told is highly unlikely you'll be granted. There is a guy sitting across from you in a restaurant, and God is telling him to tell you that God wants you to marry the woman you have been dating. Okay - that's impossible. The phone rings and what seemed impossible a second earlier just became possible.

Even now I am still in awe! Why? Because "the Holy Spirit went to lunch."

The Holy Spirit Goes to Breakfast

I arrived in Greenwich, New York on May 16, 2014 to partner with Father Tyler, the youth director at the Episcopal Diocese of Albany. I love Tyler and his wife Audrey because they're so passionate about Jesus.

Tyler and I decided to have breakfast, and the supernatural occurred. A young waitress came over to us, and then God stepped into her life. As she came to serve our meal I said to her that she was not doing what she went to school/college for. I told her that she needed to go back to school and finish her education. She asked if I'd spoken to anyone about her and kept looking at Tyler. I went on to say that she had a tremendously compassionate heart, that when people hurt, she hurt and that she sometimes became angry at injustice.

She asked me how I knew those things, to which I responded that she loved God and He loved her and that He gives gifts, and one of mine was to know things about people. With tears in her eyes she replied that she couldn't believe it. She told us that she'd started nursing school but had missed continuing on by half a point and had just been praying about whether or not she should go back.

The joy and amazement on her face was beyond words. Again, she said that she couldn't believe it. Each time she came to check on us she had an incredible glow on her face. As we sat there the Lord told me to give her a hundred-dollar tip. Listen: I COULD NOT AFFORD TO DO THIS. Normally I wouldn't have said anything but was prompted to call her over and say to her that this was not a mistake. She looked at the tip and asked, "This was not a mistake?"

She started crying and had to walk away. She stood by the coffee pot crying. After a few minutes of wiping away her tears, she came over, trying not to cry. I said, "Today, you have had a divine encounter," and added that I simply do what I am told to do and would have left a thousand dollars if I could have afforded it. Still crying, she thanked me. As she walked away, we left. I told Tyler that I could go home now.

We both agreed that her life was changed forever. Our God is incredibly amazing.

April 26, 2015: The Holy Spirit Visits a Mattress Store

That's right, a mattress store! Tonight, Troy Bourne and I ministered in a mattress store in Attleboro. Linda Amara, who used to run *Basking in His Presence* in Attleboro, contacted Troy at the beginning of the week. She had come up from one of the Carolinas and felt God wanted to do something special with some of her friends living in the area. She was so right.

Troy set up his keyboard and started to noodle, and the presence of God swept through the room. Then Linda got up and shared for a few minutes, after which all heaven broke loose. Imagine for a moment that I am in a mattress store on Route 123 in Attleboro. I remember walking in and thinking to myself, this is crazy. Linda was good friends with the store's owner, and it was he who asked Linda to have a prophetic meeting in his store. If that wasn't crazy enough, he left the front door open so the people attending the meeting could come in. Even crazier is that people who were shopping for a mattress came in, laid on a mattress, and watched a good part of the prophetic meeting.

Here are some highlights:

God spoke to a woman about her troubled life and how He was going to build a bridge over her troubles so she could get to the other side -- something she's been unable to do. The Spirit spoke to her about her indecision and how she was unsure that she was hearing from God. After the meeting, she said this was her life to a "T."

One lady had invited three friends who had never been to a meeting like this.

A young woman of twenty-three was told her life was about to change dramatically, that she had lived a very comfortable life and often chose comfort over challenge. I shared with her the story of the eaglet being thrown out of the nest. After the meeting, I was told that she indeed had had a comfortable upbringing but was now moving out of her parents' home to live on her own.

I spoke to her father and said that every time I looked at him I saw the word "healing." Then I asked, "You have cancer - yes?" Now everyone was crying. I prayed for healing. I turned to his wife and said, "You are a very strong woman and you are often misunderstood." She and her husband looked at each other in shock. Then I said, "You have a problem saying you're wrong." She started to cry and confirmed that she had a very hard time admitting this.

The Lord had me speak to another woman and tell her the story of a nurse who had deep compassion for a woman who had surgery because she had been through the same thing. I continued by saying that all the pain she is in will give her compassion for other women. She interrupted and told me that she was a nurse and went on to explain the pain of her marriage.

I turned to another woman and said that God had called her to minister to other women. I told her that she had great wisdom as well as having the prophetic insight to see into women's problems. She told me that the next day she was going to minister at a women's meeting. I responded, "I assume you have all your notes ready," and she said yes. Then I said, "Don't be surprised if God blows up your notes." She told me that just that day she'd asked God if He wanted to blow up her notes.

I spoke to a 26-year-old woman, and God said that all of her life, people were trying to squeeze her into a mold in which she didn't belong. This caused her to be rejected, but from a very young age she determined to be herself and not be pressured into being who she wasn't. I responded that as much as this was a good trait, it had caused her to be stubborn. She and her parents laughed.

All during this time Troy was noodling, maintaining the anointing. After hearing my sharing on the eaglet being thrown out of the nest; Troy began to create a song about it. It would blow your mind. What a gift to create and maintain the anointing in a room.

I walked over to a woman and said, "Write the book." She burst out, "God just told me to write a book!"

As we were saying goodnight when people were leaving, I told a woman that her whole life has been like a "roller coaster ride" and that she just wanted to get off, each day reminiscent of the movie *Groundhog Day*. I saw God applying the brakes and slowly stopping the roller coaster. She began to become very animated and then started crying. She told me that I'd "just described her whole life."

What an incredible night! Once again, we saw the truth of 1 Corinthians 14:25 where through prophesy *"the secrets of his heart are revealed; and so, falling down on his face, he will worship God and report that God is truly among you."*

That is exactly what should happen. People should be so overwhelmed that it causes them to fall down and worship and draw closer to the Lord. It should exalt the Lord and not the one prophesying. God reveals their lives, and we all stand in awe.

The Holy Spirit visits a mattress store.

May 18: Day 5 Romania

Yesterday was one of those days where I was simply speechless. In the morning, there was a baptism where I had the privilege of speaking on the topic. It's interesting how each culture has their way of explaining baptism. Without knowing some of the doctrinal beliefs of the Romanian Orthodox Church, I was able to bring some clarity without offending. Scripture says we are baptized into the Father, Son, and Holy Spirit, not baptized into a church, and that if and when we leave a church, if we were baptized in faith we need not get baptized again. The Orthodox Church, however, teaches that when you come to their church from another you must be re-baptized, the same if you commit a major sin. I told the church that the only reason for re-baptism would be if a person was originally pressured or forced into it and/or if there was no faith involved in their action.

During my sharing, the Lord spoke to a number of people. One such person was the mother of one of the young women being baptized. She had been sitting there praying that God would give her a specific word, and the Holy Spirit did just that. The worship was full of the presence of God. There at the baptism was a young lady who like a number of young people, have come to feel like one of my spiritual children. I told her how proud I was of her. Later that night she said she was speechless and felt the same way! My heart just leapt.

The second service was a baby dedication for the baby of another young woman who was again like a daughter. It was one of the most anointed baby dedications of which I have ever been a part. I presented the Godparents' Pledge which involves promising to support emotionally, spiritually, and financially. This was a new concept to the church. I had the parents pledge that they would do their best to teach their daughter about Jesus, NOT to teach her about a denomination or church, but raise her to know Jesus, another new concept.

With the event being a dedication, I wanted it to be all about the dedication and not prophetic ministry. I asked the Lord that if He wanted me to prophesy, to make it very clear. He did. After my greeting, I went to a couple and told them things only a few people knew. I don't usually ask if what I said was true, but in this case I did. With tears, they confirmed what I'd shared. It wasn't important to me but instead important to all the people visiting to know God does work through gifts. Given that there was such an anointing in the room, everyone knew something was different.

What a joy when you see the Holy Spirit touch lives!

I returned to the apartment to write and go to bed and had to rush to the bathroom. Yes unfortunately, I was very sick and found out this morning that a number of Pastor Joseph's family had the same "bug." I ached all night and still ache. Bananas and yogurt are my mainstay. Thankfully today was a schedule-free day, and I am just now feeling I can function.

It has been such an amazing time!

May 23: God Shows up at a Romanian Wedding

Good afternoon! It is 5:30 p.m., and we have just returned from the wedding, which was about an hour away. We left here around 1:30 p.m. and were back by 5:15. It was yet another experience in the Romanian culture.

The bride and groom sit on the stage after the bride is escorted by her father and given to the groom. They sit there, and no words are exchanged. The pastor and guests stand up, and the pastor brings a brief greeting, then prayer. Then at this particular wedding, there was a flute solo followed by a girl from the worship team getting up to read something to the bride and groom from a book and then speaking to those in attendance.

The program then looked like this; another pastor came and shared for about 20 minutes what was pretty much an evangelical message. The worship team sang, and then another girl got up and repeated what the first girl said.

I was then invited to speak, and Pastor Joseph interpreted. I didn't get behind the pulpit but chose instead to stand before John and Ruth to talk to them personally. I reminded them as well as the people in attendance how I prophesied their engagement before it came to pass. I spoke about the verses in Ephesians chapter five about how husbands are to love and wives to respect. I shared with them my own lack of balance in earlier days, that I spent far too much time in ministry rather than with family, and so they were to enjoy their time together. I went on to prophesy about their legacy, how they were called to work with young adults and married couples. They were smiling from ear to ear saying that they had just talked about those very things. In total, I shared around 10-12 minutes and then sat down.

John and Ruth were smiling, as we all had once again had a divine encounter.

May 27: My Romanian Trip: Another Perspective

I asked Paula, the worship leader in Brasov, to share her thoughts with you about our time together. Here they are:

We are so thankful for Brian's ministry and passion for God and for our community! In short words, his ministry here was Refreshing, Inspiring, Very Anointed and led by the Spirit.

The first three days in Brasov we had prophetic nights and many visitors came. We were impressed by the higher level of anointing in all the prophetic words Brian had from God - deeper revelations and more presence of God. It's an honor to see a man of God still growing, learning from the Holy Spirit in a humble and joyful way like Brian does. We are witnessing God's way of increasing in one person's life.

Also, his input in worship helped us a lot and helped the church enter to a new place that God has prepared and he encouraged a lot - and stretched - us, the worship team, to grasp the deeper realms of God's presence in the Congregational worship, no matter the circumstances.

Sunday morning at the service in Calan, Brian had no idea about the church or the people there, we didn't tell him anything about what was going there and the words he had for that church were spot-on. He had words that confirmed what God had spoken to this community and they were encouraged and revived by all that God has done.

Sunday afternoon was a blast! God's presence was so thick and touched so many lives. Jesus was present and lifting peoples' burdens and healing hearts. We were overwhelmed by Him!

Another thing we really appreciate about Brian is that he always was available to let God manifest how He wanted, through whoever He wanted. He didn't impose himself. And he did a very good team work with the worship team and the pastor, being sensitive to the Holy Spirit in any giving time.

Thank you so much for making possible for Pastor Brian to be here. We were truly blessed and we are really thankful for everything God worked.

Abundant blessings!

Paula and Joseph Azoica (from the worship team)

May 28: Wedding Testimony from Romania

If you remember I was asked to participate in a wedding in Romania. It was the couple that I prophesied in November would be getting married, and 10 days ago they did. During my time of sharing I had prophesied to Johnny and Ruth and asked them recently to give me feedback on the word spoken to them. Below you'll see Johnny's response.

In it he explains that a few days before the wedding he had gone to see the pastor he is under to express his convictions about their call as a couple. The pastor was critical, but later the Lord confirmed to Johnny and Ruth publicly exactly what Johnny had heard and then shared with the pastor.

Their Response:

I already had a discussion with a pastor, and he really criticized what I told him God called me to do. But the Holy Spirit was talking in my heart to let it go; He will bring people, back up, to sustain His purpose. And yes, as you told us from the Lord, we want to be a blessing for couples. And also for teenagers that are in relationships, or have sentimental issues, etc... We want to walk in God's standard. Thank you so much brother; what you said from the Holy Spirit it was true! God bless you Brian!

God Shows Up on a Dirt Road in Romania

I remember one of my trips to Romania when I was visiting Pastor Joseph's home village of Balomir. One Saturday afternoon we decided we should walk down the dirt road and invite people to come to the meeting that night. We spent the afternoon stopping to talk to people outside of their homes. It was an amazing day where the Lord prompted me to prophesy to almost everyone we met that afternoon. It was remarkable.

The result was that our meeting that night was full of people who had never attended the meetings held there. Another amazing thing that happened from our walk that afternoon was that a number of people God spoke to were from the Baptist church in the village. They were so impacted that they canceled their Sunday morning service and came to our service. I can remember the shock on the pastor's face that Sunday morning as the Holy Spirit spoke to him.

It was on this walk that we came to the rundown home of two sisters. As I looked at them I couldn't believe they were standing, never mind walking. Both of them were very old, thin, and frail, but that wasn't the shocking thing. Both of the sisters had twisted and bent legs, one of their legs going in one direction and the other in the opposite. One of the sisters was also blind. They both had a homemade crutch to help them take one small step at a time.

I am standing there thinking, "Dear Jesus, we need a miracle." We were invited to sit and then the Lord really shocked me. These severely crippled women were intercessors. They were the real deal! Pastor Joseph would visit them when he visited his hometown and would give them a number of things for which to pray. These sisters knew that no matter their condition or circumstances, they could be powerful instruments in the hands of God. (Sadly, I just found out that these wonderful women of God were murdered. The devil hates intercessors.)

It was during this walk that I met a husband and wife sitting in their yard. They were both in their 80s and looked so content. We sat down and then the man began to speak. With his voice quivering and tears running down his cheeks, he began to tell me an incredible story. He told me that shortly after they were married both were arrested for being Christians. This happened under the rule of Nicolae Ceausescu who was a brutal Communist dictator over Romania for 42 years.

As this man spoke the air was still as if the voice of God was speaking. He told me how he was beaten because he refused to tell them the names and locations of the other Christians in the village. During the time the man shared, his wife stood on a step of their front door, and tears ran down her face. As he continued all he could talk about was the goodness of God.

In describing situation after situation, he kept declaring the goodness of God and His "keeping" power. Near the end of his sharing he told me about being in jail and having a gun in his own and his wife's mouths as they demanded that the couple turn in the other Christians. He continued by saying that the Holy Spirit gave him courage and resolve not to say a word even if it meant seeing his wife murdered. As he told this story his wife wiped away more tears. The voice of God poured out of this gentle old man as he spoke of God supernaturally delivering them that day. I am still in awe!

A Supernatural Slap

After we had walked the dirt road that afternoon we had a Saturday night meeting where I was laying hands on most of the people in the room. I remember a young man in his twenties approaching me and standing in front of me for prayer. As I was standing there I heard the Holy Spirit say, "slap his head." I was thinking that that was nuts. Just at that moment however, I recalled some of the stories written about Smith Wigglesworth where God showed him to do unusual things. One was to punch a lady in the mid-section, at which point a large tumor fell out of her.

With this in my mind I slapped him gently, not hard like what is commonly known as a "dope slap." Nothing appeared to happen. It was weird, but I obeyed. A year later this young man approached me and asked if I remembered him. I apologized but said I did not. He told me that he was the man I had slapped on the side of the head a year ago and went on to tell me how prior to that night he had been continually harassed by demonic voices telling him to kill himself. He said that he was going to leave the meeting and was planning to follow through with it. Then with a huge smile he said, "But the moment you slapped me I felt something come out of me. All the torment stopped, all the voices ceased, and all the years of living in 'hell' were over."

I am not suggesting we hit, punch, or slap people. I'm just trying to encourage you to simply obey the Lord.

June 30, 2015: Last Day in Haiti

I wanted to share with you the remarkable things that God did on Saturday. In the morning, there was a pastors' meeting where I shared principles of the kingdom of God. After the first session was done all the pastors sat in their chairs, and I was thinking that it didn't go over very well One by one they got up to get something to eat, after which I thought again that it must have been a disaster.

Pastor Carlo came to me and explained that the reason the men sat there was that they were in shock. They had never heard these principles before. They told Carlo that they had to hear more about the kingdom of God, so that's what we covered in the second session. After I finished they had the same response; they just sat there for several minutes pondering what had been said. After the meeting on Sunday afternoon, two of the pastors insisted they come and have dinner with me because they wanted to hear more about God's kingdom. One pastor with a very large church wanted to invite me to it this fall.

Saturday evening, I spoke on a believer's true identity, that we were not called to be church members but instead called and chosen to be sons and daughters of God. I pointed out that the Bible teaches that we are members of the body of Christ, not members of the church. Teaching that can lead people to put their identity in the wrong thing. The pastors talked until late, expressing their regret over telling people for years that the goal was to be a church member, when all along the goal was to be born into the kingdom of God and born again as His son or daughter.

What joy I experienced from this! Reflected not only the pastors' faces, but on the peoples' as well, was the understanding of who they are and the importance of focusing on that—just that. The pastors realized they had spent their entire ministry telling people who they weren't instead of who they are. There was such joy in the sanctuary you could see it, sense it, and most certainly feel it.

How blessed and honored I was to be there. I then understood why, despite my hand injury, I had to go.

I have to tell you that when I was there I could literally feel people praying for me, and I'm so grateful that you did. Together we are changing the culture in the country.

August 7, 2015: Our Church Baptism

Today Solomon's Porch met beside a pool here in Swansea, Massachusetts. It was a gorgeous day. Rather than meeting at our church building on Mason Street, we decided to have our service outside.

A huge thank you goes to Pastor Steve, Rece, Tiana, and Mila for being such gracious hosts. Our day started with some housekeeping announcements and then worship. Imagine the presence of God showing up next to a pool! There was a brief sharing on the meaning of baptism so that everyone could understand why we follow the biblical instruction to be immersed in water. What followed was nothing short of supernatural.

Pastor Tom, Pastor Steve, and I took turns baptizing people because we wanted people to avoid the tendency to look to one man, but rather focus on being baptized into Christ. As people were baptized, the heavens opened and all 18 people received prophetic words. We see this in Matthew 3:16-17 which says, *"When He (Jesus) had been baptized, Jesus came up immediately from the water; and behold, the heavens were opened to Him, and He saw the Spirit of God descending like a dove and alighting upon Him. And suddenly a voice came from heaven, saying, 'This is My beloved Son, in whom I am well pleased.'"*

There were a number of people baptized who as we prayed and prophesied, couldn't stand up because the Spirit of God "fell on them." Others who weren't going to be baptized came under a personal conviction that today was the day, which is another reason we take time in the beginning to explain baptism. Though we had a class earlier in the week, many others came who were either not able to come or weren't planning on it. Our biblical explanation is Acts 8:36-37, *"And the eunuch said, 'See, here is water. What hinders me from being baptized?' Then Philip said, 'If you believe with all your heart, you may.' And he answered and said, 'I believe that Jesus Christ is the Son of God.'"* (You can read more of Acts eight to get a fuller understanding.)

After the baptism we ate, then some swam or sat and chatted, while others played the bean bag game called Corn Hole. Our hearts were knit together because God showed up.

August 15: Works of the Holy Spirit: Canonicus Camp - Youth Retreat

Don't look now but something is up at the summer camp in Exeter, Rhode Island. Early last night I was sitting in the back, and my eyes were fixed on a small group of junior and senior high students and their counselors. It was during the very first song that I turned to Pastor John who had once again given his time to come and be the overseeing pastor for the week. He is from a Baptist Church in Warwick.

I said to him, "Something is going on here." I told him that I could feel destiny and sincerity in the room. There was an atmosphere of hunger; these young people really wanted to be there and had hearts after the Lord. This wasn't some ordinary summer camp meeting. I could see that the Holy Spirit had personally selected these young people to come because He wanted to do something special.

The Holy Spirit changed lives forever...

March 26, 2016: Day before Easter: A Prophetic Word Given / Fulfillment the Next Day

Tomorrow is Nisan 17 or March 27. This year Easter falls on the exact date it did 2,000 years ago. All week I've been hearing that it won't be just another Easter.

Get ready, as something amazing and supernatural is about to occur. As Jesus met with his disciples early that evening so He will meet with us in the morning.

> 1 Corinthians 2:4-5 (NKJV): *"And my speech and my preaching were not with persuasive words of human wisdom, but in demonstration of the Spirit and of power, that your faith should not be in the wisdom of men but in the power of God."*

> 1 Corinthians 4:20: *"For the kingdom of God is not in word but in power."*

So, the question is, do we want a nice safe service where we all sing, hear a message, and then go home, or do we want the Holy Spirit to do amazing and supernatural things?

Will we celebrate a day called Easter or will we become those who carry the Spirit of Easter? Safe or supernatural? The Pharisees didn't mind so much when Jesus taught, but boy did they get upset when he walked in power. Yes, Jesus taught, but He spoke with power.

Will this Easter be an Easter to remember? Will people leave our services having their faith be in the wisdom of man or in the power of God?

March 27, 2016 – Easter: Works of the Holy Spirit: The Holy Spirit Came and Breathed on Us: The Only Condition? Receive it, or as the Cambridge Bible says, "Take it"

Yesterday was a supernatural day. The Holy Spirit walked into the sanctuary at two services. Yes, I said two services. At 10:30 we met at the Porch, and at 12:30 I was in a Spanish church on Pleasant Street. The guest speaker at both services was the Holy Spirit.

As in John 20 Jesus walked through the locked door into the room the disciples where hiding in. Yesterday Jesus walked into two churches and changed all of our lives.

Many of us had areas that we have kept locked. But yesterday Jesus unlocked those doors.

As the disciples were filled with fear, we too are often held captive by our fears. But then yesterday, Jesus walked into our lives and replaced our fear with peace.

Where people were hopeless, He breathed hope. Where there was despair and depression He breathed on people and overwhelmed them with His love and affection.

As Jesus was in a tomb, yesterday Jesus set people free from their own personal tombs that they might enjoy life.

Jesus showed his disciples his hands and his side. Yesterday He came and invited us all to have a greater revelation of Him. A spirit of revelation filled the room and our lives.

As Jesus said to them, "as the Father has sent me I send you," yesterday Jesus anointed people and sent them out to preach the Gospel of the Kingdom.

Yesterday the power of God swept through both church services. People wept, and they crumbled and fell under the power of God.

I was honored to be a part of this supernatural Easter, yet while I don't want to seem unthankful, I don't want to live in yesterday. The Lord spent yesterday setting us free -- healing our wounds, imparting hope, and giving us a deeper revelation of Him.

Why? That we may not only live lives filled with peace and joy but that we could be His sons and daughters declaring His goodness to those to whom He sends us.

Works of the Holy Spirit: More News from Easter

Yesterday in the afternoon I called the man who translated for me on Easter Sunday at the Spanish church. Whenever I minister in another church I typically call the next day to see how they felt about the ministry and if they have any questions.

When the translator answered the phone, he was very exuberant. He was talking so fast that I had to repeat what he was saying so I wouldn't misunderstand what he was communicating. The funny thing is that when he answered he called me Bishop, which is how the pastor introduced me to his church on Sunday. He used that term because of the churches I have planted and my itinerant traveling. It is so funny to hear it.

Anyway, he told me that the pastor and the entire church were blessed with what the Holy Spirit did on Sunday. He spoke about being on the floor (he was there for a while) and the Holy Spirit showing him a number of painful episodes that had occurred in his life as a child. He went on to say how the Holy Spirit healed his heart. He was not aware of how these episodes had profoundly affected his life.

In his broken English, he spoke about his wife, who is the worship leader. During the time, I was praying with her you could see the Holy Spirit touching her, yet I knew that the Lord wanted to go even deeper. So, He told me to take off my suit jacket and put it on her shoulders. As soon as I did she collapsed, and her husband spoke of the things that the Holy Spirit had done in her life. Her life was transformed by the power of God. I also want to say that the word of God transforms our lives as well.

In our own church (the Porch) both Pastor Tom and Pastor Steve told me how they could feel the power of God flow out of them. When I watched the video of the service, the Holy Spirit on Pastor Tom was visible. As we spoke about Easter he told me how the prophetic words he was speaking just penetrated people's lives, and many simply broke down. He was literally seeing lives supernaturally changed in a few moments as people stood there in front of him.

When I spoke to Rece who was on the platform, she told me that no one remained in their seats, that everyone was in the aisle waiting for prayer. She reported that in all her years she had never seen a response like that. Remember -- this was Easter Sunday.

I can't begin to tell you the joy that floods my heart when I hear of all the things the Holy Spirit did on Easter. To be an eye witness of the transforming power of the Holy Spirit is so overwhelming that I just have to raise my hands and worship him.

We want to declare what Paul writes in 1 Corinthians 2:4-5 (NKJV), *"And my speech and my preaching were not with persuasive words of human wisdom, but in demonstration of the Spirit and of power, that your faith should not be in the wisdom of men but in the power of God."*

Can I have an amen?

You Can Make a Difference: April 8, 2016 Haiti

It has been an incredible morning. Pastor Carlo arrived with another pastor, and we had a great breakfast. As we talked Pastor Carlo was reflecting on last night and how waves of the presence of God swept over everyone as we worshipped. He asked me if I had heard the pastor of the church weeping in the corner.

I spoke to Carlo what the Holy Spirit had told me to share for Sunday morning. (Their service starts at 6:00 a.m., and we have to drive an hour to get there). The Lord showed me how because of voodoo, people are afraid of the power of God, afraid of the baptism of the spirit and speaking in tongues. Many times, as I would pray with people and the power of God would hit them, they would run away from me.

In the 21 years, I have been coming here, I have mentioned voodoo but never spoken against it directly until now. The spirit has stolen people's identity, their inheritance, the anointing, and the power available to them. I am to wait until Sunday to teach people the need to renounce voodoo. I will take the two services prior to Sunday to develop a relationship with them so when I do speak about renouncing voodoo they will have built a trust and a relationship.

When I spoke to Pastor Carlo about what I was going to share he started shouting, "Wow, wow, wow! "He said that Leogane, the city we were in, was Haiti's capital of voodoo and yet I wouldn't have known this. Where we had parked the truck the night before in fact, was on the land they held meetings and sacrifices. Carlo continued to say "Wow!" and told me that God had given me a secret key. Imagine God having me wait until He brought me to the capital of voodoo before I spoke against it, just as Jesus had done in cursing the root.

Okay, it's 6:47 EST or 5:47 here in Haiti. I've been back in my hotel room about a half an hour. I came in, changed out of my dress pants, shirt, and tie then packed my suitcase. I have to leave here at 5:00 a.m.to catch a 7:03 flight to Miami which then goes on to Boston.

Let me tell you what God did today. We arrived about 7:40 and went into an over- crowded church. People kept on coming in and then they began to stand outside. Their worship had changed, and as Pastor Carlo closed the service with worship, you could see how much the Holy Spirit had done in just three meetings.

After worship and two choirs I was asked to come and speak. The Lord had me prophesy over the pastor, as he had said at lunch, he had felt something come on him. One of the choirs sang about the glory of the Lord being on them. That morning while preparing for the service the Lord directed me to Isaiah 60:1-3. It says, *"Arise, shine; For your light has come! And the glory of the Lord is risen upon you. For behold, the darkness shall cover the earth, And deep darkness the people; But the Lord will arise over you, And His glory will be seen upon you. The Gentiles shall come to your light, And kings to the brightness of your rising."*

I so want to encourage you to embrace the reality of these verses. This is God's word to each of us. Go back and reread it and then declare that you will walk in this prophetic promise.

I stood up and told the congregation that God had prepared this word for them. I went on and told them who they are and how honored I was to be among a people who love God and are pursuing Him despite living in horrific conditions. I began to tell them that in the 21 years I have been coming to Haiti that I had never directly attacked voodoo. I went on to say that Satan is a thief (John 10:10), and he had stolen from them truth, peace, joy, and their inheritance. I spoke about Acts 19 and 2 Corinthians 4 in verse two about renouncing the hidden things, renouncing meaning to sever or cut. I tied a small rope on me and Pastor Carlo held the other end of the rope. I then tried to move forward and could only take a few steps because I was being held back because of my involvement with false teaching in college, when on a few occasions I had called on the dead. These were spiritual ties that I needed to renounce. Finally, as I was pulling away from Pastor Carlo, the rope was cut, and I was free. Who the son sets free is free indeed.

People were engaged during the entire time I was speaking. I had their full attention and there were no, and I mean no, hindrances. As I ended I asked them whether they might also consider renouncing false teaching and the spirit behind it, to renounce witchcraft as mentioned in Acts 19. Then I suggested that perhaps they might want to do this right then, in the moment. I had Pastor Carlo take over, and he prayed and asked people who wanted to be free to come. Not everyone came, as it was a lot to take in at one time, but the seed was planted. Perhaps half or a little more than half of the people, did come forward, however. Near the end a couple of young girls crumbled to the cement floor. Thank God for His presence.

I had a hard time leaving because many came forward to thank me. Only God can do these things. We left there and went to visit two pastors. Then we drove back to Port Au Prince to have lunch with another pastor and his wife. The food was great as was the fellowship, and God showed up!

So, my time in Haiti has ended. Thank you again for your prayers and financial support.

Works of the Holy Spirit: Michigan April 27, 2016

There is a song I love called "When He Walks into the Room." This is exactly what happened here last night in Holland, Michigan. I am so in awe of how a room can be totally transformed from being ordinary to one where God is tangibly present. It is like when Moses and Joshua would meet with God in Exodus 33:9 and it says from the New Living Translation: "whenever Moses went into the meeting tent, the cloud would come down and stand at the door of the tent. And the Lord would speak with Moses."

An ordinary room becomes a tabernacle of meeting. Literally God steps into the room and yes, "Everything changes." If you want, here is the song "When He Walks into the Room." It's worth a listen! https://www.youtube.com/watch?v=8Zqg5k_GUx4.

I am so blessed to have Troy Bourne with me again along with my nephew Tim Haney and his daughter Annani. When they began to sing the room was transformed. You don't have to come to a meeting to experience God; you can meet with Him wherever you are!

One way we can experience the presence of God is to worship with sincerity. In 2 Kings 3 Jehoshaphat needed to hear from God, so it says in verse 15 that he made a particular request: *"But now bring me a musician. Then it happened, when the musician played, that the hand of the Lord came upon him."*

There was the ebb and flow of worship and prophetic words given. So many amazing words were spoken, which only God can do. I emphasized that people didn't need to attend a meeting to hear from God, nor did they need a man/woman to speak for God, that they have the same right and privilege to hear from God themselves.

I'll share two highlights from last night. One was that Troy sang a song he had written on the plane from Providence to Grand Rapids which captured much of God's intention for the three days we would minister. It was amazing. The other was that there was a young woman in her early twenties whose aunt had invited her to come. It was her first time at one of our meetings. God told me to speak to her as if I was her father. As the Lord spoke to her He told her how special she was and how proud He was of her, continuing to lavish His love and affection on her. The young woman burst into tears. I was and am still amazed how much He loves us.

So many other things were spoken, and over two hours flew by. How blessed and honored we all were to be in His Presence.

I pray that you can meet with God today.

An interesting thought came that in Exodus 33 when anyone wanted to meet with God they had to go outside of the camp to the Tabernacle of Meeting. Exodus 33:7: "and it came to pass that everyone who sought the Lord went out to the tabernacle of meeting which was outside the camp."

The point is that they had to make the effort. If you listen you can hear Him calling you to come.

Works of the Holy Spirit: Michigan April 29 - Wow!

I woke up this morning in awe. One of my favorite expressions is "ONLY GOD." Last night at 7:00 when we were supposed to start, no one was there. I said to myself, "Okay Lord, what is your voice in this?" There was no answer and then young people started to come into the room. Then more young people and still more young people arrived. Within 10 minutes the room was filled with young people, the majority of them from 18 to the mid-20s.

I have done a number of youth meetings but never has the Holy Spirit designed a meeting where God's intention was to minister to the young men and women who God will use for the next generation. I became so excited to see and be a part of mentoring the next generation of Davids, Nehemiahs, Daniels, Esthers and Deborahs. The meeting took on more of a mentoring atmosphere, which was incredible. What an honor to be part of God's plan for the next generation.

There were so many amazing moments. I spoke to one young man who listened and tears came to his eyes. He turned to the person who brought him with his mouth and eyes open wide and a look of shock on his face. He'll never forget the night when God supernaturally revealed himself to him. There was a young lady who I saw as one of the servants who helped prepare Esther to become queen. Her delight is doing all she can to see other young women reach their fullest potential, making them "beautiful" for the Lord. There was also the call to do missions and then eventually lead mission teams.

There was a young man who was crying a lot whose emotions were all over the place. I told him that he was a type of Jeremiah, who had been known as the weeping prophet. I told him that at this point in his life he is not a prophet per se but has a prophetic gifting. I said, "You often pick up on the emotions of others around you. You can feel sad, confused, angry, and disappointed, and what you thought were your own emotions were actually the emotions of people around you. He was so relieved by this word, because he had been bewildered and had no idea why his emotions seemed so convoluted.

Imagine the joy that Troy and I had to watch God's divine plan unfold before our eyes! So much more was done by the Holy Spirit. The meeting ended at 9:15, and people lingered, talked, and prayed with one another until about 10:30. No one wanted to leave, because the presence of God was so palpable.

Works of the Holy Spirit:
Michigan April 30, 2016 - Still in Awe

It's Sunday afternoon at 12:23, and our flight back home was canceled because of the weather in the Providence area. Due to the cancellation, we went to a church in Jenison called Solomon's Porch. It was good, but I really miss our own Solomon's Porch.

Last night Troy, Tim, and I finished our ministering at Intersection Ministries in Holland, Michigan. A huge thank you goes to Lauretta (Rett) Deboer for all of her labor and to Jim Shelter for his three nights of service. I also want to thank the leadership of Intersection Ministries for opening their doors to allow us to come.

Last night was totally unique compared to the previous two nights. The verse that is so imperative for us is 1 Samuel 10:7: "Do as the occasion demands; for God is with you." Every time we minister we have to discern/discover what God wants to accomplish and how He wants to go about it. It is critical that these things are considered each and every meeting.

The night was filled with worship and prophetic words where we could see lives being transformed before our very eyes. It is so incredible to see how the Holy Spirit molds, shapes, and changes lives in mere moments.

As the night was drawing to an end I felt there was a need to pray with people who wanted it, and as I prayed with people, the power of God would overwhelm them. In fact, there were a number of small children who fell to the floor when prayed with as well as numerous adults who didn't get up for several minutes.

Yes, Paul was right when he wrote in 1 Corinthians 4:20 (NKJV), *"For the kingdom of God is not in word but in power"* and 1 Corinthians 2:4 (NKJV), *"And my speech and my preaching were not with persuasive words of human wisdom, but in demonstration of the Spirit and of power."*

Yes, I am still in awe!

Romania: June 3, 2016

It is now 10:25 p.m., and I just returned from our first service and from having dinner. I had breakfast with Pastor Joseph at 8:00 a.m., and then he left me to do some work. It wasn't long after that

I had a bout of running to the bathroom every five minutes. Because of this I canceled my afternoon with him and used the time to pray, study, muse, worship, and nap.

Pastor Joseph picked me up at 5:30. The evening service started a little before 6:00 and went until 8:00. God allowed me the opportunity to prophesy to a number of people including two pastors. When I started speaking to them I didn't know they were pastors but started declaring that they were and spoke about the challenges they were facing. Pastor Joseph blurted out that they had just been talking about what I had finished prophesying to them about. There was such joy that filled the rest of the room, and they responded to what was spoken with such delight.

During the afternoon while musing with the Lord He told me to tell them, "I am about to do something that will require a new way of thinking, perceiving and seeing. He showed me Habakkuk 1:4 where God speaks to Israel and says, *"Look among the nations and watch - Be utterly astounded! For I will work a work in your days which you would not believe, though it were told you."* He went on to say to tell them, *"that their tomorrow doesn't look anything like their yesterday."*

He continued to speak through Joshua 3:4, *"For you have not passed this way before."* Everything that they have known and lived will not equip them for their tomorrow. He spoke to them (and is also speaking to us) that our journey is going to require truly being led by the Holy Spirit, that using our natural mind will not work in the days ahead.

God said, "Don't make the mistake that Israel made in Numbers 13" when God sent twelve spies into the Promised Land. While all twelve saw the amazing things that were in the Promised Land, ten of them were consumed with the obstacles. We too can see how amazing our tomorrow is, but like them we see and are hindered by the obstacles. The roadblocks we see become greater than the God we can't see. Remember what God first spoke to them (us), that it will "require a new way of thinking, perceiving and seeing."

Our tomorrow awaits us, and so do the obstacles. Our tomorrow is filled with wonder and awe. We haven't been here before. It will require really being led by the Spirit, not by the things we have done in the past. Jericho was defeated one way but the city of Ai required a different strategy. What works or worked in one situation will not work in the next.

God spoke to them and is speaking to us, "Get ready to be astounded."

Romania: June 4 (Part 1)

I have a little time before I'm supposed to go out. It's 9:25 a.m. I was awoken at 4:00 with a phone call from Haiti that I didn't answer but responded to by text. Since I was awake, I called my wife who I hadn't talked to since I left on Wednesday. It is always a joy to hear her voice. She has sacrificed so much for the Kingdom of God.

We chatted until about 4:30. I sent a few more text messages and then went back to sleep until 6:30. I got up, put the coffee on, and finished yesterday's summary. Somewhere in the middle of the night I had asked the Lord what he wanted to say at tonight's meeting. He responded with, "It's going to take supernatural answers in our tomorrow."

Honestly, we are so naturally-minded, and our first response to any question, problem, obstacle, or for just about any situation is to look for answers in our natural mind. But it's difficult to receive supernatural outcomes by using natural methods. We just have to laugh at ourselves for thinking we can.

Think with me for a minute about all the supernatural answers we have missed, and praise God that He works beyond the limitations that we erect, that He works beyond us! Despite this, imagine what could happen in each of our lives if we began seeking supernatural answers, answers which exceed the boundaries of this world. That ought to excite us!

What an incredible tomorrow we all have! How about inviting the Holy Spirit to remind us to step out of our natural kingdom and enter the realm of our Father's Kingdom. You know, "Thy Kingdom come, thy will be done on earth (again, ON EARTH) as it is in heaven." There are supernatural answers and insights which are available to us. It's part of our inheritance.

Off to do some musing and then out for the day.

Romania: June 4 (Part 2)

Its 10:55. I just got in the door from an evening service that started at 6:00 and ended a little before 9:00. We lingered for a while and then went and had dinner at Pastor Joseph's house. I am not sure how much I will write tonight because I am very tired.

The anointing was very powerful. A woman from Germany was there who is working with the church to help them understand prophetic intercession and how to pray for their city and Romania. She spoke before me for about 40 minutes. Then I got up and shared and prophesied for a little more than an hour. The room was packed. I'll see if I can download a couple of pictures. I never take pictures, but Pastor Sajeev from India (who is the pastor who interpreted for me while I was there years ago) prompted me to do so, and I did.

Its 6:00 a.m. I was so tired I wrote just a bit and then went and sat in a chair just to decompress. All of a sudden, I heard all kinds of noise outside and could see the reflection of blue lights flashing and assumed it was from a police car. I went to the window and was able to sit on the ledge of the window. As I looked to see what was causing the noise, the sky was being lit up by fireworks. It was spectacular. There was no delay between the fireworks being shot off; one after another after another came.

A thought came into my mind that there was a meaning/voice from God in the fireworks display. The fireworks continued, and I asked the Lord what it meant. He said, "It's a sign of celebration for the work that I am doing in Romania, and this is just the beginning!"

Shortly after this I went to bed and slept for six hours, which was much better than my nightly average of a little more than four.

So back to a brief recap of the service. When I got up to minister I had a sense that I would only have a few prophetic words, which was true. I told the packed room that I might not have a personal prophetic word for them but had a word from the Lord for everyone. One of the words I spoke was to a young man with whom I had spent part of the day. He and a young lady who is one of my daughters here in Romania took me to see a castle and to have lunch, and our time together was very meaningful. I told him that God speaks to him from the time he gets into bed until just before he falls to sleep. I went on to tell him that he needed to have a writing tablet and pen next to his bed so that when God whispered to him he could write it down so he would remember. Just as I finished he spoke out that he does, in fact have a writing tablet beside his bed to write thoughts and ideas that come to him in that "twilight" time.

Then there was an older woman sitting in the corner whom the Lord spoke to with such affection. I saw her sitting at a table in the morning during the harsh, communist rule eating a bowl of oatmeal and praying. Day after day she would pray as she saw many people die. I told her that her prayers were among those which brought an end to the communist regime in Romania. I can't tell you the joy that filled me as I spoke to her.

The word I spoke to them was the same word I spoke the night before, which was that God was about to do some incredible things in Romania, and He was asking them to be a part of it (read Habakkuk 1:5). Again, the Lord spoke about not having been this way before (Joshua 3:4), that it would require a new way of thinking, perceiving, seeing, living, and a willingness to be truly led by the Holy Spirit. I also said that our level of effectiveness will be in proportion to how much we live in the Spirit and not in the natural man. I quoted 1 Corinthians 2:14 CJB: *"Now the natural man does not receive the things from the Spirit of God."*

I shared with them that there were supernatural answers for many of the obstacles/giants that presently existed and that they would face in the future, that all of us had tried to resolve our times of adversity by using our own natural mind. I shared how Gideon was told to go and defeat the Midianites, who numbered more than 120,000 men. When Gideon had 32,000 men, God told him he had too many and that those who were afraid should go home. Twelve thousand were left, and God told him he still had had too many. He instructed him to have them go to the river and drink and send home those who lapped the water like a dog instead of cupping it. He did as he was told (as we should) and was left with an army of 300 men. <u>Then</u> it was time to go to war.

There are supernatural ideas available for all of us, but it requires not living in the natural. I could go on, but you get a sense of what God is doing. Thank you again for praying for my time here in Romania.

Surprised by the Holy Spirit: June 25 - 26 Plainville, CT

It's almost 10:30 p.m. on Sunday night. I returned home this afternoon after spending yesterday afternoon and this morning at Holy Trinity Anglican Church in Plainville, CT.

YES, YOU READ THAT RIGHT! It was an incredible two days!

I had the privilege of watching the Holy Spirit touch the lives of a remnant people who had never seen prophetic ministry. Seeing God move within a very traditional church which has no background or understanding of prophetic ministry literally takes your breath away. For two days, I witnessed the Holy Spirit step into a room and turn lives upside down, which caused all of us to be in awe of the Lord.

In 1 Corinthians 14:24-25 it says that when an unbeliever or an uninformed person comes into a room and hears someone prophesying they will be convicted and *"the secret things in their heart will be made known (verse 25, ERV). So, they will bow down and worship God. They will say, "Without a doubt, God is here with you.*" Yes, the purpose of prophetic ministry is to have people draw close to the Lord, which in turn brings them into a place of greater intimacy.

Over and over again I was asked out loud, "How do you know these things?" After a time of worship Saturday afternoon, I came to the front of the altar and turned and started prophesying to the worship team, person after person. The first man God spoke to heard that he was like Jacob and continually wrestles with God. He said, "This is so true. I wrestle all the time and have so many questions to ask." The young man beside him has never fit in; he was continually rejected by his peers, and God then told him why. The Holy Spirit also spoke to him about his wife and his call to do youth ministry. You should have seen the joy on everyone's faces.

I then spoke to the worship team about the difference between praise and worship. I had them slow down the tempo of the song "Good Father," sing it more dynamically, and do so *to* God rather than *at* God. As they did this the atmosphere changed, and everyone felt it. During this session and the one on Sunday (it's now Monday morning) not only did I prophesy, but I was able to lay some foundation of truth and to mentor people as well. I told them that their goal was not to live for the purpose of going to heaven but instead to rule and reign with Christ here on earth. Yes, we will go to heaven, but that is not our eventual destination, earth is. We spoke from Genesis one about how we were created to govern.

They sat there with their mouths open. They were nodding their heads saying," We see it." Much of the time we spoke about their true identity and their true purpose. People began to see their value and who they were and began to stop looking at who they weren't. They were discovering that they were "God's masterpiece." (Ephesians 2:10)

The Lord spoke to one woman about being an encourager and loving to be alone with God. While this was wonderful, it tended to be a place where she would hide because of all the rejection and abuse she had endured. Over and over again she asked," How do you know these things?" She then blurted out about how her father abused her for years, at which point I was able to speak about forgiveness, release, and blessing.

It was such an honor to share principles of the kingdom of God, in essence the fulfillment of Ephesians 4:11-13 (NKJV): *"And He Himself gave some to be apostles, some prophets, some evangelists, and some pastors and teachers, for the equipping of the saints for the work of ministry, for the edifying of the body of Christ, till we all come to the unity of the faith and of the knowledge of the Son of God, to a perfect man, to the measure of the stature of the fullness of Christ."*

After Saturday's session Father Jim and his wife Ginny told me that many people came as skeptics and even for the purpose of exposing prophetic ministry as fake or disingenuous. In fact, a very prominent person came to me and said this exact thing. The buzz in the room Saturday afternoon was electrified after our time of laying hands on just about everyone. You should have seen their reaction as people were touched powerfully by the Holy Spirit, so much so that on Sunday morning there was an excitement and anticipation in the air!

Jack Deere wrote a book years ago called <u>Surprised by the Holy Spirit</u>. This weekend that is exactly what happened!

Romania - November 10, 2016

It is 8:00 a.m. on Thursday morning. We drove two and a half hours from Brasov to Bucharest yesterday to the home of Stephan and his wife and his extended family. He was the key person to help sponsor the Pastors' conference in Brasov.

We arrived here, had lunch and quiet time and then were off to a meeting with pastors, leaders, and students. It took us an hour to drive a short distance because of the incredible amount of what they say is normal traffic here in the city of Bucharest. We arrived at the church, and initially there was no keyboard for Troy, but then they pulled one out.

We started ministering a little after seven. The Holy Spirit had me weave teaching and prophesying for just over two hours. Then for the next two plus hours I prayed and prophesied over just about everyone in the room.

I continue to be amazed at how God knows people and lets them know that He does. Over and over people stood, cried, laughed, and stared in amazement. There was a teenage girl whose hand I took, and the Lord said, "I want to give you joy." He talked to her about her sadness. A woman stood behind her weeping. When I finished she said, "This is my daughter, and her entire life she has been sad." She said that it had broken her heart to have such a lovely daughter who was always sad. On and on the Holy Spirit spoke to people. One young man was told he didn't need another word but instead needed to meditate on and activate what God had already spoken to him. He admitted that while he sat there waiting for prayer that the Holy Spirit had already told him that very thing. What a wonderful night.

Romania - November 12, 2016, Part 2

It's 10:08 p.m., and we just arrived back in Brasov after about a six-hour ride. On the way here we did stop in Bucharest for dinner with Stephan and his wife.

I have been coming here for six years now, and I continue to learn not only about the Romanian culture, but about their church culture as well. It is so important to understand both so I can more effectively help impart the culture of the Kingdom of God. It's important to understand the culture God is replacing.

Over the weekend, for example, I was with over 200 Romanian youth who had all came from Pentecostal churches. Rather than clap or raise their hands, they had been taught to stand and worship in reverence. In addition, for the most part they do not interact with the speaker. When I first asked for a response and didn't get one, I thought that perhaps they didn't get it or that I was totally off the mark. Thankfully as we continued to minister, however, the cultural walls began to come down.

For today's sessions, we broke into two groups of about 100 or so each. One way to impart a new culture of God's Kingdom is to walk up to a few teens and prophesy about their lives. Immediately you get the attention of the room.

When I was introduced Friday night I was presented as someone who had a prophetic gift. I had no leading to prophesy, but I thought it was important for them to see that gift in operation so that they would know the gift is real, but more importantly so they would realize how intimately God knows them.

It was during the last sessions that the Holy Spirit prompted me to prophesy. I spoke to one young lady who was sitting beside a young male. God showed me they wanted to get married and when they did they were to open their home and host young people. I told her that the person she wanted to marry was a bit of a clown and always having fun. Many who knew them couldn't help but look at each other in amazement. Another young man was encouraged to stop comparing himself with others, that God loves him just the way he is and to not be concerned about someone else's opinion of him.

In another session, I told a young girl that her being bilingual would be a huge part of her future. I also saw the word medical and that she would travel. She especially wanted to go into the jungles but was not to pass up going to a nice island, that ministry doesn't always have to be hard. She told me when I was done that she interprets for medical teams. She wanted to go into the jungles of Africa and recently turned down a medical mission to an island.

I saw a second young lady writing with a desire to publish books. I went on to tell her not to listen to all the negative voices that speak to her. I finished and asked her if this was true, and she and her two friends with huge smiles replied, "Yes, one hundred percent!"

The message to everyone is that God is real and that He knows and loves us.

The meetings were not about personal prophecy per se but much more than that, about being part of a generation that would turn Romania upside down. With that as the purpose of these meetings, I shared how God wants to use young leaders.

Romania - November 15, 2016

It is almost 7:00 a.m., and I am sitting in the airport. I went to bed about 1:30 and got to sleep somewhere close to 2:30. I slept until 4:50.

It has been an amazing trip. I was blessed last night to minister in a small but vibrant Gypsy community. The person leading worship did a tremendous job in leading us in intimate worship, which is very unusual here in Romania.

As we were sitting there before the meeting, a man walked by me, and I turned to Pastor Joseph and Stephan and told them that the man carried authority and leadership on him. Stephan responded and said that he wasn't the pastor. I responded that there was no doubt that he carried leadership and authority.

Well who do you think got up and opened the meeting? The moment he opened his mouth he was in charge, and the pastor who had come into the room was very glad to let him lead.

We started at 7:00, and I finished sharing and prophesying around 9:00. Then Pastor Joseph and I prayed for people. We finished somewhere after 10:00, and by God's affection and grace, He spoke to everyone.

After the service, we went upstairs and Stephan prayed for healing for an older woman. When Stephan prays, though I don't understand a word he says, I can feel the strength of his anointing. A mother had gone home to get her daughter and as we were leaving, God spoke to her in a radical way. She knew that God had spoken to her. It was wonderful.

As is the Romanian culture, we went out to eat with the pastor of the church and his wife and children. He had such a sweet spirit. He was a dad, and the people really loved him. After the meal, the pastor began to share with enthusiasm, but once again, I didn't have a clue as to what he was saying. Thankfully Marcel who had rejoined us, interpreted for me. He said he had never seen anything like it, that it was extraordinary and "excato," meaning each word fit each person exactly. He went on to say that he listened to every word spoken to every person and said it was 100 percent correct. His comments were almost word for word the phone call I received that afternoon from the pastor where we had ministered Wednesday night.

It's always very gratifying and humbling to hear that kind of feedback.

Prophesying to Mayors

I have had a unique opportunity in the past four years to be in a position to prophesy to four mayors, two in Fall River, Massachusetts and two in Romania.

It was three plus years ago when Pastor Joseph of Brasov, Romania was invited along with 40 other pastors to the mayor's office of the city of Brasov. He had called them there to try and obtain their support for the upcoming election. It was forecasted that he would lose because the other mayoral candidate had the backing of the president and other high-ranking officials. The mayor asked everyone to introduce themselves. After that was finished there was some chit chat, and sadly a lot of the pastors were like male dogs peeing on trees to claim their territory. It was embarrassing.

I turned to Pastor Joseph and told him I had a word for the mayor. Pastor Joseph waited to say something to him. You have to imagine that the room was filled with Plymouth Brethren, Baptist, and other traditional pastors. We were the only charismatic pastors in the room.

I stood up and told the mayor that he was going to win the election because God called him to be an instrument of blessing for the church. I went on to tell him the story of King Cyrus in Ezra 1:7-8 (NKJV): *"King Cyrus also brought out the articles of the house of the Lord, which Nebuchadnezzar had taken from Jerusalem and put in the temple of his gods; and Cyrus king of Persia brought them out by the hand of Mithredath the treasurer, and counted them out to Sheshbazzar, the prince of Judah."*

The mayor's lawyer was there, and he and the mayor looked at one another in shock. The attorney stood up and said that one of the reasons the mayor had called them to his office was to announce that the land that had been taken from the churches during the communist rule of Nicolae Ceausescu would be returned to the churches.

I am still in awe of what God did that day.

A few minutes later I told Pastor Joseph that they needed someone to anoint the mayor. I didn't say that I should be the one, but I felt that I should. Fifteen minutes went by, and the mayor stood up and asked me if I would come and anoint him. Immediately you could feel the tension in the room. Joseph and I went over to him, and I anointed him with oil then prayed and prophesied over him again. When we were done the animosity in the room was evident. They were angry that a Pentecostal American not only prayed, but had the audacity to prophecy.

I know the mayor won reelection, though I am not sure as yet whether he has returned the land.

Another mayoral encounter occurred a year and a half ago when we were in the city of Hateg. We had gone into a local hotel to use their Wi-Fi, and within a few minutes the mayor walked in. When I was introduced to him I began to prophesy. He smiled and said he had to run but asked if we could come see him in an hour. We went to his office an hour later, and he wasn't back yet so we decided to leave. On the way out, however, he walked in and insisted we come to his office. He told me that he was a believer. I interrupted him to prophesy. Then Troy Bourne who was with me sang a lengthy prophetic song over him. Troy finished and the mayor wiped tears from his eyes and then confirmed the accuracy of what was spoken and sung. Amazing stuff!

Here in Fall River, Massachusetts we have had three mayors in the last two years, and I have had the opportunity to prophecy to the last two. Both of those occurred in a restaurant. The first mayor I spoke to sat there stunned, and the man with him said that everything I had just said to him was true.

The second prophetic word I actually wrote out and handed to the mayor at the lunch that Pastor Tom, Pastor Steve, and I had with him. He hasn't responded yet.

Indeed, you do not have to be on a mission's trip to have God use you!

Miscellaneous Michigan Trips

On one of my trips to Michigan I was invited to a Dutch Reformed Church. I had been speaking to the pastor on the phone trying to discourage him from having me come, but he kept on insisting that I should come to his church. Over and over I told him that it probably wouldn't be a good idea because it would create problems for his ministry. He continued to insist, so I went.

When I walked into the church I waited in the foyer to meet him and saw him come through the sanctuary. As he came over to me, I heard the Lord say that "a year from now he won't be in this church." (It was probably 10 months later when he stepped down and left to work with youth because that was where his passion was.)

I stood up after worship and shared the scripture where Jesus said, "let's go to the other side." I then approached 12 or 15 people and standing three or four feet from them, prophesied to each one. I remember telling one man that he had a special relationship with the pastor. Everyone knew (except me) that indeed he had a father/son relationship with him, and after the service I found out that he had adopted the pastor as a father, and the pastor had adopted him as his son. The pastor had a stern look on his face as I was prophesying to him, because he didn't want to convey any emotion. This didn't last long, though: multiple tears began flowing down his cheeks, one after the other.

I found out after the service that I had prophesied to nine of the 12 elders on the eldership board. They thought that I knew who they were and that someone had somehow told me all about their personalities, their gifts, and their callings. I didn't know any of that, but God did.

I remember one night when we were meeting in Zeeland, Michigan and there were so many divine encounters. Many of the people who come to these meetings come from a Dutch Reformed background. They are lovely people who really honor the word of God.

There were so many nights that the power of God showed up. We saw multitudes of people baptized in the Holy Spirit, many of them overwhelmed by His power as they lay on the floor. There were pastors who came to these meetings wondering if prophesy and the power of God is real. There was one night that I identified one such pastor.

We met at his office the next day, and he told me that he came not believing in the things of the Spirit but left fully convinced that they are real. He told me that no one knew the things I spoke to him and that he did everything he could to resist falling down to the carpet. He was on the carpet for over 20 minutes.

On another night, the Lord spoke to a couple about needing a vacation. I saw a blue truck with an extended cab that was stuck in the mud. It was a prophetic picture of where the man and his wife were in their lives. They looked at each other and told me I'd just described their truck. As I was speaking to them the Holy Spirit told me to give them a week's vacation from my timeshare.

Wedding Reception

I was attending my niece's wedding reception when the Lord told me to go and speak to a particular couple. The husband happened to be a pastor. For 30 minutes, I prophesied to him and his wife. They told me that I had just summarized where they were in their lives and that they so needed to hear it.

Being Willing

This brings me to a place where I want to encourage you to be willing to step out and take risks. Over the past number of years, I have seen the value of 1 Samuel 10:7 where it says, *"do as the occasion demands; for God is with you."*

I have a close friend named John Polce who is a very gifted guitarist, singer and song writer. He and I have ministered together a number of times. He often recalls the night I asked him to go with me to a Black Pentecostal Church. Normally the music in these particular churches is very "enthusiastic," lively, and loud. Just before the service began, however, I turned to him and asked him to do the song "This is the Air I Breathe." John looked at me as if I had two heads and thought I must be joking.

To this day he laughs and says he has never seen anything like the presence of God invading that church. The pastor told me later that they hadn't had the presence of God like that in years and years. The message: be willing!

I can't begin to tell you how many times during services the Lord tells me to give money away. On a recent trip to Canada I saw a couple and after prophesying to the wife one night and the husband the next, I was told to give him $100 to take his wife out. This has happened countless times. In the same meeting, I was speaking to a woman and was told she was a missionary and that she needed funds to go on her next trip, so I reached in my pocket and gave her $50. This has also happened on more than one occasion!

Grocery Stores

I can be in a church service or in a grocery store; it doesn't matter. For a period of two years I would go into a store and the Lord would say, "Pay for their groceries." I remember the first time I was told to do that. I was behind this woman and heard, "Pay for her." As she was reaching into her purse I handed the clerk the money, and he told me that it was her order. I said "Yes, please take this." The woman turned and asked me why I was doing it. I told her that the Lord wanted to show her how much He loved her. She burst into tears and after a moment said, "I thought he had abandoned me, and this was the only money I had." She gave me a big hug and then left.

The clerk said to me, "It's nice you can afford to do that." I replied with a smile on my face and said that actually I couldn't afford to. He asked me then why I did. I told him that as Christians we are told to love people and to minister to those in need.

There were so many times this happened, so I finally asked why. I was told "that if I could be faithful in little I could be faithful in much."

There was this afternoon that I was bagging my groceries and saw this older woman with very thin hair. I heard "Pay for her groceries." As she reached into her purse I gave the clerk $60. The bill was a little more than $54. I didn't stand there and wait for the change, as I was hurrying to leave the store. Out of the corner of my eye I could see the clerk point to me. The woman came over and began to scream, "What did you do that for?" I said, "God wants to say, He loves you." She then asked if I was a minister to which I responded yes. Her response was hilarious. She said, "Then it's okay then." She turned and walked away.

I have been led to stop in stores and say to people, "Excuse me. I was standing over there and I believe the Lord spoke to me about you. Could I share with you what I believe the Lord wants to say?" I have learned to get permission first. How did I learn that? There was a time I was in a pharmacy line and didn't get permission, and the person ran out of the store.

I was in a hurry in a grocery store and as I walked past this woman, God gave me a download. I stopped and shared it with her. She thanked me, and off I went. As I was cashing out the Lord said, "Go tell her this…" I questioned the Lord and asked him if He was sure. I left my bags on the checkout counter and had to search the entire store to find her. I really didn't want to do this, but obedience is the key. I found her and shared. She smiled and told me that I had no idea how critical it was for her to hear that that day. She informed me that she was what is termed a "Holy Ghost preacher," a person who preaches with a fiery anointing.

Airplanes

I love to fly and always pray that the Lord gives me someone to talk to. It has often been mothers who God speaks to about their children. There was one flight where I saw more than I wanted to and was afraid my ministering to this woman could be misinterpreted. I saw that she had just gone through a painful divorce, that her husband had been unfaithful, and that she just wanted to love someone. Her son was in prison and her daughter was a mess on drugs. I told her all these things, and she became extremely emotional. The plane was delayed in landing which allowed me time to finish speaking to her. I prayed for her and couldn't wait to catch my connecting flight.

On a return trip to Boston from Miami once I sat in business class. For three and a half hours God spoke to this man who was a believer but didn't believe in the gifts of the Spirit. I never told him my address or church's name. That wasn't important but seeing his life transformed was. I saw that this young man was in college and told him which one and also his major. He was also involved in a "male" relationship. God spoke to him about his pain and how it had led him to make wrong choices. I never mentioned the relationship but spoke to how he could be healed.

There are countless times that I have been willing to speak to people. That's one of the keys to being used by God – our willingness.

There are times I want to minister but God doesn't. I was on an aisle seat and a couple sat beside me. I asked them what they did for a living, hoping they would in turn ask me. They finally said, "So what do you do?" I told them that I worked for my father in the restoration and reconciliation business. They never asked me to explain. I was willing, but God wasn't.

Watching God Heal

I've seen so many amazing healings and miracles! I've seen God do things that simply took my breath away. I remember visiting a Gypsy village in 2015 and going from house to house. In each home, I would prophesy to everyone there. In this one home I prophesied to a man about his governmental authority and his influencing the community. After I had finished he told me that he was the chief of all the Gypsies in that region and had been working with the mayor on trying to establish policies and procedures.

At his house, I prophesied to everyone but this one young girl who was sitting there rather quietly. They asked if I was going to prophesy to her, and I said that I wasn't but that God told me that he wanted to heal her. At that moment, everyone in the room began crying. I didn't understand why until they told me that she was blind. I got up and walked over to her with Pastor Joseph and one of his elders. I laid my hands on her and spoke a short word of prayer. Within moments a strange look came over her face, and she turned to her mother and said, "Mommy, I can see!" Someone who witnessed this actually used their cell phone to capture the whole event. The link is:

https://www.youtube.com/watch?v=g3gVXp_dVKO

People ran from the home and through the entire Gypsy village declaring what God had just done. We then decided to hold a spontaneous meeting that evening in the center of the village. It was something you read about in a book. As we began preaching, people came running from all over the village. They swarmed to the platform, and that night dozens of men and women gave their hearts to the Lord.

The Holy Spirit in a Hair Salon

I so want to encourage all of you to be who you are, wherever you are.

For at least fifteen years I've had the same hair stylist who owns her own hair salon in Fall River, Massachusetts. I can't begin to tell you the number of times that God has had me minster to people in her salon, the gifts of the Spirit not always for just inside the church but very much for outside as well. Each one of us can sow seeds which bring people closer to Christ and encourage them that God not only loves them, but has a plan for their lives.

I remember one day I saw a woman in the salon who was really struggling with a variety of difficulties. The Lord told me to pay for whatever services she received, which included a cut and color. I asked how much it was, and the total was a lot more than I wanted to spend, but the issue is always obedience. The woman was so blown away that when she got home she called the salon to tell them that she was coming back in so she could in turn bless someone else by paying for their hair services.

I have also seen God move in healing in the salon.

Healing is for Today

I have had the privilege of watching God work through so many people in the gift of healing. Since 1981 I've seen countless people who were in such pain be supernaturally healed. I've seen God heal people in church, in stores, in restaurants, in parks, on planes, near swimming pools. I've seen cancer disappear, tumors shrink, hearts, backs, trauma, diabetes, bipolar disorders -- all healed, and the list continues.

Years ago, I knew a man who had a severe head injury and was told by doctors that he wouldn't live. As I stood in his hospital room I saw that he was hooked up to a number of tubes, including some attached to his brain. I was wondering whether or not to pray. The thought came to me that there was nothing to lose, so I prayed a simple prayer which was by no means earth-shattering. I didn't yell, shout, or holler. I just prayed like all of you.

The result was that he miraculously lived through the night and over several weeks improved enough that they sent him to a special brain trauma hospital. Since the original prognosis was that he would never recover, as is protocol, they took away all his legal rights and gave them to his wife as his proxy. It was perhaps a year later that he walked out of the hospital having regained them all. I was told he was the first person to ever get his legal rights back.

A few years ago, we were putting on a community outreach in the church parking lot when a homeless man wandered in. After talking with him for a while he divulged that he was an alcoholic. We asked him if he wanted to stop drinking, and he responded that he did. We began to pray with this man, me remembering past prayers for those addicted to alcohol. I prayed specifically that each time he took a drink it would taste like gasoline.

He left and I never saw him again until a year later when we were hosting another community outreach in the church parking lot.

This man walked up to me and asked if I remembered him, which I didn't. He proceeded to tell me he was the man we had prayed for a year earlier. He told me that the afternoon we had prayed for him and every time after that when he tried to drink, it tasted like gasoline. He told me that the year previous he was living in the woods in a tent, but today he had a job and an apartment and oh yes, he had made Jesus his personal savior. Imagine: one simple prayer that you pray can start the process of turning a life inside out and upside down – YES, <u>YOU</u>!

> *"Be ready to do it whether it is convenient or inconvenient."* 2 Timothy 4:2 (CEB)

One of the things the Holy Spirit is encouraging us to do is to be willing to respond to what He shows us he wants us to do "in the moment." Two other translations for 2 Timothy 4:2 are: *"Be ready in season and out of season."* (NKJV) and *"Be on hand with it whether the time seems right or not."* (CJB)

You've heard it time and time again that faith is spelled RISK. Will you make mistakes? Yes, but God is bigger than your mistakes.

In the baseball world, there is something called the Baseball Hall of Fame. This is where the very best baseball players are recognized for their lifetime achievements. There are many baseball players in the hall of fame with a battling average of three hundred or less. A three hundred batting average means that out of 10 times they have gone to the plate to hit they have only gotten three hits.

Thank God that with Him our average can far exceed that!

When we go on vacation I love going to the pool to read, study, pray and to see if God wants to speak to someone. I remember I was at a pool in Florida, and God began telling me that this man had just had a divine encounter, that he was a businessman about to embark on a very big venture. He also said that He was trying to get this man's attention, that he needed to be less involved with business as it meant neglecting his family.

Put yourself in my bathing suit (haha). Do I say something or not? I wrestled with whether I would or wouldn't. Finally, I got up and said, "Excuse me; I know this is going to sound peculiar, but I was over there, and I believe the Lord wants me to tell you something."

I told him what I had heard, and he told me that on the way there he and his family were in a serious car accident and according to the police, he, his wife, and son should have all been killed but not one of them was injured. He spoke about a friend who told him exactly what I said to him just before he left for vacation. He affirmed the part about business and the need to put his family first. He had barely finished speaking when he began to pick up his things, and as he was leaving said, "I have to go call my friend."

"Be ready to do it whether it is convenient or inconvenient."

Poolside in Arizona

I was inside our room while vacationing in Arizona, and it was 7:00 in the morning. I heard, "Go to the pool and prophesy to the man there." It was already close to 100 degrees, so off to the pool I went. Sure enough, there was a man there by himself. I asked the Lord what to say, and the Lord said, "Go, and I'll tell you." In Psalm 81:10 (NKJV) it says, *"Open your mouth wide, and I will fill it."*

I approached him and began telling him that he is a senior pastor in a large church and was there considering what to do. I continued by saying that there were many members of his board who wanted to fire him because he had begun to see things about the gifts of the Holy Spirit he had never seen before.

He was dumbfounded. He told me that he had just arrived and was there at the pool to consider all the things I had just said to him. I never told him who I was, because that's not important. I said instead that I would pray for him, and as I walked off he said in a very loud voice, "THANK YOU!"

While I am writing this, I hear that I am meant to say THANK YOU for all the times that you responded to the Lord and took a risk.

The Holy Spirit in a Hotel Lobby

"The wind blows where it wishes, and you hear the sound of it, but cannot tell where it comes from and where it goes." John 3:8 (NKJV)

Donna and I got to spend a night here in Providence celebrating our 45th wedding anniversary. We had a great dinner then went back to our room where I promptly fell asleep. Can you say tired? I am clearly still recovering from my eight-day trip.

In the morning, I went downstairs to get a cup of coffee (yea Starbucks). I also needed to check out, and one of the people checking us in last night was still there. That seemed very unusual because it had been 13 hours. And guess what happened? The wind of the Spirit started to blow. We begin chatting, and then the homeless shelter came up, which in turn led me to tell the woman how I met Jesus.

She started crying while her co-worker was meanwhile listening to everything. Imagine standing at the service desk of the Biltmore Hotel, and the Holy Spirit is there!

She began to tell me of her journey and her anger with God --the tragic stories of her childhood and all the pain she had been through. She is still in the process of recognizing her anger with God and realizing she needs a relationship with Him. God was so gracious to her by providing her with a mentor, which I want to encourage each of you to be as well -- people who mentor by word and deed. She kept on touching my arm and crying. The wind of the Spirit was blowing. I told her that I didn't always understand why God allowed certain things, but I knew He redeemed everything. I shared the principle of forgiving and releasing, her co-worker again listening to every word. I was with them for over 30 minutes.

Whatever you have been through will become bread for the hungry and water to those who are thirsty. Oh Father, thank you for your continued redemption. Over and over again you take our tragedies, our mistakes, and our sins, and you use them to bless and heal others.

I came back to my room rejoicing that God's "wind" was blowing in a hotel lobby. I wasn't led to pray with them, yet as I walked away I could see the Holy Spirit capturing their hearts and minds. I am confident that the words we speak are like arrows which piece the soul.

Lord, I pray we can discern the blowing of the wind.

The Holy Spirit Visits Spas

During my recovery from my second back injury I discovered that scar tissue can be broken up through massage therapy. My first visit to a spa just a few miles from my home afforded me a meeting with a wonderfully-gifted massage therapist. As she began to delicately massage the area where scar tissue had built up, the Holy Spirit began to speak to me about this very sweet and tender young woman.

As I began to speak to her I felt hot tears hit my back. She didn't say a word but the tears said it all. At one point, she had to stop and compose herself. While she was a Christian and knew about prophecy, she had never seen it operate in an everyday setting. The Lord spoke to her about her past, her present, and her future. She heard how the young man she was currently dating was not the man that God had chosen for her. As much as she knew this, for her to think of another failed relationship was extremely difficult. God spoke to her of another man who would be her Boaz.

There were other occasions when the Lord spoke to her. One afternoon during a massage I said, "Well, you and your boyfriend have broken up." She was shocked that I would know that. Happily, Boaz came within a short period of time. She wanted to invite me to the wedding but didn't want to cross the client/patient barrier. I fully understood. Later the Lord said, "You will move away," and months later I lost a tremendous therapist.

It took a while before I found another therapist, and guess what happened? Yup, the Holy Spirit came crashing into her life and spoke to exactly where she was at. What the Lord said to her affirmed and strengthened who she was and gave her the determination to go forward. Thankfully she is still my therapist today. Oh, and the Lord has ministered to her children as well.

Just down the road is my chiropractor who I'm also blessed to have. Her particular technique was one of the contributing factors in my getting well during the sabbatical I took in 2008. Over the years during my appointments God at various times has stepped into her life as well.

The point is that we all can be used by God in very diverse environments with very diverse individuals. Whatever your gift is, please use it. God has equipped you to be His representative and His ambassador. Second Corinthians 5:20 (CEB) says, *"So we are ambassadors who represent Christ."*

God Moves Wherever He Wants

I have seen God move in Episcopal churches, Baptist churches, Faith churches, Dutch Reformed churches, Anglican churches, Independent churches, Assembly of God churches, Pentecostal churches, Black Pentecostal churches, Evangelical churches, and Catholic churches.

One of my fondest memories is when I was with Father Jake Randall, a great man of God who many believe was the father of the charismatic movement in Massachusetts and Rhode Island. When we had our first prophetic meetings at Solomon's Porch in 2009, I invited him to come and minister in our first meeting. It was powerful.

I also had the opportunity to be with him at Lasalette Shrine in Attleboro, Massachusetts and at other times with John Polce. We saw lives transformed in literally a few minutes as God moved through the prophetic word and with power. Our Father loves people and fulfills His word. As it says in Matthew 18:20 (NKJV),

"For where two or three are gathered together in My name, I am there in the midst of them." God is bigger than our theology, and He is also bigger than our prejudices and our small-minded thinking.

There is a saying that goes like this: Where does an 800-pound gorilla sit? Answer: Anywhere he wants.

Our God is bigger…

God Shows Up at St. Charles Catholic Church in Providence, Rhode Island

On June 15, 2013, I was invited to minister at St. Charles in their English-speaking service which has between 50 and 70 people in attendance each Sunday morning. On the Brazilian side, well over 1,000 attended.

It was a Thursday night, and I was there with John Polce, who was doing the evening's music. This prayer group (40 people on this particular evening), had been dwindling in size since the passing of Father Randall, and in fact they are still grieving his passing. Only God though, can "give us beauty from ashes and a garment of praise instead of mourning."

I arrived early and sat in my car to pray and worship. As I did a man got out of his car, and as he was walking past me the Holy Spirit spoke to me about him. Later that night when I finally ministered to him EVERYONE in the room was UTTERLY AMAZED. Honestly, I continue to be astounded after a meeting because of all the Holy Spirit does.

For two and half hours the Holy Spirit spoke distinct detail to each person addressed. The lead priest attended a good portion of the meeting and yes, God had a word for him. When he came forward for prayer he knelt and raised his hands. God moved on him so powerfully that as he knelt, the power of God knocked him over. The meeting ran late, and after he told me that I could then be counted as a pastor of his parish. What an honor!

The next day he called the prayer group leader to get a copy of what God had said to him. God spoke to him about being promoted with the diocese. He was shocked because just two days earlier he had indeed been promoted to an executive role within the diocese. No one knew except the bishop and a few other priests.

In the evening, the head deacon sat in the back of the room thinking that the whole prophetic ministry was a farce. He was about to leave when I began to speak to him. What God spoke only he knew, because he had never shared his feelings with anyone.

That night people laughed, cried, and gasped as the Spirit moved. John opened with very anointed music, and during the time he ministered I would stop him so I could share a prophetic word, and then John would play again. I like to mingle worship with ministering so that we can all remain focused on Jesus and not get caught up in the one giving the prophetic words. Our focus must always remain on Christ. After the service John shared with me that he knew all the people God had spoken to, and he said that it was like I knew them. Well, I didn't, but the One who loves them does.

What I didn't tell you is that when I was sitting before the service began I looked around the room. As I did, the thought came to my mind that it was going to be a short night, because with my natural eyes I couldn't see the gifts and talents that were present. I saw nothing but people. Sadly, at this point I did not have God's heart for these people. Oh Father, give us your eyes and your heart for people. Help us to see them as you do!

You might be asking yourself why I was at a Catholic church with all their wrong theology. The very thought assumes your own theology is perfect and has never changed. Sure, there's a lot of theology in the Catholic church I don't agree with, but that is true of a lot of places I minister. All of us are being transformed, and yes, through the years our theology stretches and shifts, yet we were, are, and always will be believers in spite of that. PRAISE GOD!

Good News Chapel:
An Evangelical Church in Attleboro, Massachusetts

November 23, 2013: One of the ministry leaders had received permission to hold special nights of prayer, so I was invited along with John Polce to come and do prophetic ministry in a church that in general does not believe in the gifts of the Holy Spirit. It is important for me to share that the senior pastor/elder knew I was coming and that that was my purpose. He even popped in for a minute.

Picture that I am at a prayer night with an entire room of people who don't even believe in prophetic ministry. As usual we had to create an atmosphere where people recognized the presence of God in the room even though they might not be able to articulate it as such. As John was creating an atmosphere of intimacy, they did know that something very wonderful and different was taking place!

I watched in amazement as the Holy Spirit spoke to person after person about their lives and their gifts and talents. People laughed and were amazed and shocked when the Holy Spirit spoke to them specifically and personally about their lives.

Here was evidence once again of the Holy Spirit crossing denominational lines and boundaries to reveal Himself and His love for His children.

Saturday Night at Solomon's Porch: Fall River, Massachusetts

It is November 19, 2013, and we are on the second floor of my home church hosting our bi-monthly prophetic night. This particular Saturday night we had over 100 or so people gathered to meet with God, most of them not from our own church.

Every life that came to this little place in the middle of nowhere had their lives imprinted by the Spirit of God. There was no big-name speaker, but the person we all wanted to encounter was there – the Holy Spirit. We worshipped, and His presence filled the room. In that alone we all felt loved, cared for, and special, our hearts encouraged, burdens lifted, and sorrow removed, with joy filling our hearts. All this and more occurred in WORSHIP. People discovered a greater place of intimacy, so what was meant to be a two-hour meeting lasted for over three.

We watched the Holy Spirit dramatically and directly approach people and saw the fulfillment of 1 Corinthians 14:25 where *"the secrets of his heart are revealed."* People wept; they were filled with unspeakable joy, given supernatural insight, wisdom, and healing. They heard the voice of their beloved and were built up, edified, comforted, and encouraged. For over an hour and a half God's Spirit blew on people's lives much like Ezekiel 37. People wept and laughed, and we knew we were in the presence of MAJESTY… A woman who is an intercessor and continually lays down her life for others, drove all the way from Woburn, Massachusetts, almost two hours away, to bring a man she knew who wasn't a believer, but certainly left as one. She too received a number of words from the Lord that filled her heart and soul.

We saw the Holy Spirit place new anointing on people's lives for the tasks ahead. King David was anointed three times – once at age 17, which empowered him to step into the next phase of his life and ministry, then 13 years later as he was anointed in Hebron so he might govern one tribe, and finally seven years later when he was anointed to govern all 12 tribes from Jerusalem. As with him, with every increase in calling and responsibility, God has anointing for you.

I would say that only a few people didn't come for prayer, and that the power of God fell over the whole place.

If that wasn't enough, many people were healed. There were words of knowledge that were spoken about various medical issues, and God touched lives.

Hearts were knit together, and we all left with a deeper love for the Lord and a deeper desire to serve Him. Yes, our God dramatically changes lives.

God Visits Christ the King Healing Center:
An Episcopal Retreat Center

Today is July 24, 2012. I was honored to minister to an amazing biblical remnant of Episcopal priests, leaders, and people from diverse backgrounds. Every Tuesday they have a healing service led by Father Nigel Munford, who is a wonderfully gifted and anointed priest. These services are always full.

The service began at 10:00, and I preached, prophesied and prayed from 10:30 to 12:30. The worship minister was a woman I have been blessed to minister with a number of times at the Healing Center. I prophesied to the retired and also the out-of-retirement Bishop of Albany. Father Nigel kept saying how wonderful and accurate the words were, and people applauded. There were well over a hundred people there.

I spoke to priests, a nun, deacons, lay leaders, and many others. I walked over to a couple and told them that the missionary anointing was on them, but it wasn't to foreign lands. After the service, the wife said they were educators and were called to missions with children here in the US. I spoke to the husband and told him that I saw a baseball dugout and that he had been sitting on the bench, but God was filling out the lineup card. He was going to have the husband bat first in order to be the person who sets everything up, and he would therefore never go back to the bench. He then shared that he was a baseball coach! The place erupted.

The entire time the presence of God engulfed us. After creating what's called a "fire tunnel" for prayer, people came to me individually, everyone that is, except the last girl who was on the floor. The baseball coach had never been to a healing service, and when he was prayed for, he hit the floor in amazement. When he got up there was a need for a man to catch all the other men who were on the floor. He told me that he'd never seen anything like that in his life. One woman said that she'd been coming for eight years and had never seen such a move of God. Another said they'd seen people fall but never like that.

Such an incredible day. God steps into a room and says I LOVE YOU. The message centered around Mark 16:20, "And they went out and preached everywhere, the Lord working with them and confirming the word through the accompanying signs." It is our commission to go everywhere... and the Lord will work with us confirming the gospel with SIGNS AND WONDERS.... It doesn't say "they worked;" it says God WORKING WITH THEM....

Hebrews 2:4 says, *"God also bearing witness both with signs and wonders, with various miracles, and gifts of the Holy Spirit, according to His own will."* God will back you up – we are entering into the new thing God is doing. It's having confidence as His children that He will accompany you no matter where you go, and He will allow you to be as Paul when he said in 1 Corinthians 2:4-5, *"And my speech and my preaching were not with persuasive words of human wisdom, but in demonstration of the Spirit and of power, that your faith should not be in the wisdom of men but in the power of God."*

IT IS YOUR CALLING TO DEMONSTRATE THE SPIRIT AND POWER!

Our Prophetic Team Visits Haverhill, Massachusetts

Today is May 31, 2014. Today our worship team less one -- Pastors Steve and Tom, Dan, Lisa, Rece, and I -- traveled an hour and a half to minister to a church's leadership team. It was amazing. It was a day of activation as we went as a team to do prophetic ministry. And that is exactly what happened – we truly worked as a team.

There were prophetic worship and songs, and Lisa even sang over a woman (Zephaniah 3 says that God rejoices over us with singing.). As she and Rece sang, the woman was totally undone – ONLY GOD CAN TOUCH A LIFE LIKE THAT.

Pastor Tom stepped into a greater dimension of prophetic ministry, having a number of life-changing words for people. Pastor Steve has himself reached another level of powerful prophetic ministry. At one point after we had finished officially ministering to someone, I turned and saw Dan, and I knew that he also had a word for him, and wow, did he. Later on, Dan had another prophetic word – how exciting is that?! Dan had never publicly prophesied (perhaps had never prophesied at all), and he did it with such ease and accuracy. Lisa and Rece even came off the platform to pray and minister to a woman on their worship team.

We started about 10:00 a.m. and finished near 1:15 p.m. or so. There were times when a brief prophetic word was given and people just fell backward to the floor. This occurred in Jesus' ministry when they came to arrest him and He asked who they were looking for. They said "Jesus". He said, "I am he," and all the soldiers fell backwards to the ground. It just shows us what power is in the spoken word.

I have never seen or been a part of an entire team ministering prophetically as one until now.

P.S. This past April 22, 2017 this same team returned to Haverhill, and once again, OUR GOD WAS FAITHFUL.

God's Protection and Provision

By the time this book is published I will have celebrated my 68th birthday. That will mean I have had the privilege/honor to have walked with God for 48 years. In that time, I can tell you that God has always been faithful.

From reading this book you might think that I have always made the right choices and done the right thing, but in no way is that the case. In fact, if you were with me right now, you might hear me chuckle!

Indeed, He is always faithful even when we are not.

Very often God will use circumstances and situations to take us deeper in Him and continue to refine our character. Gold and silver is refined by fire. In 1 Peter 4:12 (NKJV) Peter writes, *"beloved, do not think it strange concerning the fiery trial which is to try you, as though some strange thing happened to you."* It's all part of God's master plan. In 2 Timothy 2:20 (NKJV) we read, *"But in a great house there are not only vessels of gold and silver, but also of wood and clay, some for honor and some for dishonor."*

In this life-long journey our Father has prepared for us, one of the greatest things we can learn is how to be content in whatever circumstances we find ourselves. Paul writes in Philippians 4:11 (NKJV), *"Not that I speak in regard to need, for I have learned in whatever state I am, to be content."*

No matter the circumstances you will discover that God will protect you and provide for you.

In Need of a Financial Miracle

Like many of you, the last number of years has been an opportunity to trust God for my personal finances. The last few years our church income has really declined due to people moving away, people becoming unemployed, the reasons go on. Since we planted Solomon's Porch there was never enough income to receive a full-time salary. To be honest I have no idea how we have continued to pay our personal bills. I have always held to the conviction that I should always pay the church bills first before taking a salary. Last year our income declined even more, and at one point we were several months behind in our mortgage. Like Jehosephat in 2 Chronicles 20 I didn't know what to do, but my eyes were on the Lord.

Our pastors and also my wife knew that we were behind in our mortgage, but they weren't sure how much. Unless God did something, we would lose our home. To be honest I was expecting a foreclosure letter from the bank. A letter did arrive from the bank but instead of saying they were going to foreclose, they offered to redo my mortgage at no cost and to extend the years on it as well as to roll what I owed back into the mortgage at my current interest rate. My mortgage payment dropped over $900.00 a month, and at the same time I applied for Social Security, the amount I was paid more than covering my mortgage.

What happened with the bank was truly a miracle. I've never heard of a bank sending a letter like that. This is the third time God in his kindness has kept us from losing our home.

It didn't happen because I was a pastor. It happened because like you, He loves me. He didn't do it because I am perfect. He did it because of His great kindness. I am not sure what the future holds, but this I know this: He loves me.

God Involves Himself in All Our Needs: I Needed a Car

Last May when Donna's car lease was up I began exploring the dealership that would offer us the best price for leasing a new 2016 Honda Civic. After speaking to a number of dealers, I settled on one. While there I inquired about trading in my 2014 Honda Accord because it had too many miles on it for my lease, but to get out of it was going to cost BIG MONEY. So, needless to say I agreed to get a new lease for Donna and to pass on my car.

I told Donna about the deal, and she responded by saying that I needed to try another dealer she mentioned. Happily, I listened and went and negotiated her getting a new Civic for less than 15 dollars more than what she was paying. I asked about my car, but it was crazy money. Donna and I went the following day and with no money down and less than 15 dollars a month more for a three-year upgrade, I was happy. They asked me about my car and how much I was willing to put down. I said I couldn't afford to put any money down and that I wasn't in a position to increase my car payment. Three times they asked me how much I wanted to put down. Three times I told them I couldn't do it. Finally, the salesperson said to the owner, "I want to get this pastor into a new car." The owner told him to do whatever it took.

So, with no money down and less than 15 dollars a month, we drove out of the dealership with two new cars. Oh, and an important detail is that my credit isn't very good because of the sharp decrease in pay I've taken over the last few years.

You can see that God works on our behalf. He makes a way where there is no way. We don't need money; we need Him. He knows our needs.

This book has been written to encourage you that the Holy Spirit does lead, teach, and guide us. In John 14:26 it says that the Holy Spirit "will teach" us and in John 16:13 that He "will guide" us. The Holy Spirit wants to move in our lives, but He requires each of us to respond to what He shows us.

God Protects Me from the Mafia

In the late 70s before my back injury prevented me from working, I was employed by a man who was connected with organized crime. I didn't know it when I started working for him, though. I had never sold before and was desperate for a job. With no sales experience, I believed everything I was told by the owner. I started out having great success but soon realized that much of what I was saying wasn't true. Instead of quitting though, I stopped lying. My sales plummeted, which created a tension between us. He didn't know I wasn't misrepresenting his product anymore.

One morning I was sitting in the office when he received a phone call. His son who was a realtor in Boston had just evicted a man from an apartment. This man called the office and threatened to hurt his wife. As my employer heard this he literally turned red in the face and hung up and made a phone call. He asked the man on the other end what he was doing that night. A few days later he told me that the man he'd called had found the man and broken his legs.

After this we got in his car, and I saw a blood-stained baseball bat in the back seat. We ended up going to a job site where a man was shingling a roof. The man came off the roof and told my boss that he couldn't put new shingles on because the plywood was bad. My boss said, "Just shingle the roof and don't worry about the plywood." He told him he wouldn't do it, to which my boss replied, "If you don't shingle the roof you'll never climb a ladder again."

I began to pray about how I could quit. Within a day or so the car that that I was driving had its engine seize. I called the man I was working for and said I couldn't come in. I told him that since my sales had fallen off I wasn't able to pay my bills. He told me to bring in all my bills and that he would also buy me a new car. I told him thanks, but no thanks. He then said, "You owe me." At this point I was scared but had to trust God.

To make a long story short, I trusted God to protect my wife and my kids. And the outcome was that God protected us as we fully trusted Him. I never returned to work though the man called me again and again.

God is faithful whatever we are going through.

God is Omnipresent

Like all of you, I can look back on my life and see where God has saved me from being severely injured or killed. The message of John 10:10 is a reality, not just some words that John the Apostle wrote. Here is what it says in the New King James Version: "The thief does not come except to steal, and to kill, and to destroy. I have come that they may have life, and that they may have it more abundantly."

There are multiple times when we are protected from car accidents. Numerous times in high school I would sneak out and party and while driving would lose control of the car. Someone else would take over the driving, however, and I never got into an accident. I would do 360s in the middle of the road. While traveling on an interstate outside of Salt Lake City I hit black ice doing 65 mph and went down a very steep embankment. The car should have rolled over but didn't. Another time I drove home from work and fell asleep on Route 95 near the Foxboro exit and woke up some five miles later at the Mansfield exit, the car traveling straight ahead about an inch from the guard rail.

I had 2,000 pounds of brick fall on my back and lived; I fell two stories off scaffolding and landed on my back yet was not seriously hurt. Sure, I had a severe back injury, but I was supernaturally healed twice, once after five years, the second after seven. Oh, and the things I learned!

I had my life threatened by a Mafia "enforcer," and I told him that he had no power over me unless God allowed him to have it. I also worked for a man who was "connected" and after a serious incident occurred, I became aware of these connections and the potential consequences for my own life. Not wanting to know more and to work for him any longer, I quit. He responded by saying, "I treated you like a son, now you owe me." The details are unimportant; what is critical is how God protected me.

I rejoice in Luke 4:10 (AMP), *"For it is written and forever remains written, 'He will command His angels concerning You to guard and protect You.'"*

The Holy Spirit and the Family

It would be impossible to write about all the times the Holy Spirit spoke to me about our family. Often, He would tell what my kids were doing, but looking back, I wish I had spent more time asking Him not only what they were doing, but also what they were thinking. If I had known their secret plans I might have prevented certain situations. Countless times the Holy Spirit would tell me what Donna wanted me to bring home or something that was on her heart, and then lo and behold, I would show up with it.

There were numerous times when my daughter Crystal was in college that we would visit her and very often take a handful of her friends out to eat. On each of those occasions God would have me prophesy to them. I would go around the table and God would speak to them about very personal things in their lives. Many of her friends saw that God was real, and because of that a number of them committed their lives to Christ.

Seeing the Supernatural within the Natural: March 18, 2017

Tonight, was another supernatural night. By the natural eye you would not see the moving of God, but oh how incredible the working of the Holy Spirit! Tonight, we saw God appoint a man (Pastor Tom Mello) as the senior pastor of Solomon's Porch of Fall River, Massachusetts. That alone should take our breath away. Imagine for a moment an ordinary man and his wife Lisa who both love God. At the age of nineteen Tom knew that God was calling him. Little did he know that some twenty plus years later God would entrust him with the leading and caring of a people who would recognize him and his wife as the "shepherds of their lives."

It was supernatural because in 2009 the Lord led me to plant my third (and last, I hope) church. As the Lord led me to plant the church, I knew that the day would come that God would reposition me, and I would release the church into the hands of another. I didn't actually give the church away, because I never owned the church.

As I had written earlier, I had started Judah Christian Fellowship in 1995 in the same city. The Holy Spirit had given me a three-year plan, but out of exhaustion I released the church after only one year. I mention this because this time I learned from my past mistake (disobedience), and I waited for God to direct me as to when I should release it. I just love how the Lord gives us new opportunities to glean from the things we have learned.

It was a supernatural night also because a church was entrusted to another to impact a city. It was a supernatural night, as I must trust God to show me what to do. You see, very often we miss a very powerful move of God because we are looking for signs and wonders that are in fact, quite obvious. We see an example of this in 1 Kings 19:11-12 (NKJV): *"Then He said, 'Go out, and stand on the mountain before the Lord.' And behold, the Lord passed by, and a great and strong wind tore into the mountains and broke the rocks in pieces before the Lord, but the Lord was not in the wind; and after the wind an earthquake, but the Lord was not in the earthquake; and after the earthquake a fire, but the Lord was not in the fire; and after the fire a still small voice."*

Your life will be so very different when you can discern the supernatural in the natural.

The Word of God is Supernatural

As I am finishing this book it is crucial that I declare and make plain that I so deeply appreciate and am so thankful to see the power of God move on the earth. Equal to that, however, is the WORD OF GOD. Though I have spoken on all the supernatural things I have seen, I must also testify that for over 45 years I have seen lives restored and healed, sinners become saints, marriages restored, families reconciled, and life after life transformed by the Word of God.

Hebrews 4:11 (ERV) says, *"God's word is alive and working. It is sharper than the sharpest sword and cuts all the way into us. It cuts deep to the place where the soul and the spirit are joined. God's word cuts to the center of our joints and our bones. It judges the thoughts and feelings in our hearts."* Psalm 119:105 (ERV) says, *"Your word is like a lamp that guides my steps, a light that shows the path I should take."* Without the word of God, we indeed would have no foundation and be left instead to our own reasoning and imaginations.

Second Samuel 22:31 (NIRV) says, *"God's way is perfect. The Lord's word doesn't have any flaws."* How can each of us fulfill Romans 12:2 without the written word of God that says, "And do not be conformed to this world, but be transformed by the renewing of your mind, that you may prove what is that good and acceptable and perfect will of God."

I have seen people healed, delivered, changed forever, and entered into eternal life simply by reading the written word of God.

Final Thoughts

In conclusion, I hope that you have seen that He is the God of highs and the God of lows, the same God during times of great joy and great sorrow. He is always present.

Though at times it doesn't feel that way, He is always loving. He will see us through whatever we face, though at times it may take years. While we live and breathe and have our being in Him, we very often will not feel His presence, but instead may even experience the enemy of our soul harassing us. On occasion, I have to remind myself that I am not called to live by feelings but by faith.

I love this scripture from 1 Kings 20:28: *"A man of God came to the king of Israel with this message: "The Lord said, 'The people of Aram said that I, the Lord, am a god of the mountains and not a god of the valleys. So, I will let you defeat this great army. Then all of you will know that I am the Lord, wherever you are!'"* Yes, our

Father is God no matter where we are or what has happened or will happen in the future.

God was my God when we had no funds and I didn't know where we would find the money to buy milk, diapers, or toilet paper. He was and is the same God when we were debt-free and didn't lack for anything. He is the God of lack and the God of plenty. Like Paul, however, I must learn the secret of contentment. It says in Philippians 4:11 (NKJV), *"Not that I speak in regard to need, for I have learned in whatever state I am, to be content."*

I trust you noticed the term "learned?" Indeed, I am still learning after all these years.

We are like Aaron's rod. When his rod was placed in the temple it supernaturally budded flowers and produced almonds. In Numbers 17:7-8 (NKJV) it says, *"And Moses placed the rods before the Lord in the tabernacle of witness. Now it came to pass on the next day that Moses went into the tabernacle of witness, and behold, the rod of Aaron, of the house of Levi, had sprouted and put forth buds, had produced blossoms and yielded ripe almonds."*

This is a prophetic picture of us. We are natural people, but when God touches us we become something extraordinary and are transformed into available instruments in the hands of a loving God who wants to reach the world and has chosen us to do just that. Though imperfect, we are people who are being transformed into His likeness.

It's almost a running joke that when we go to a restaurant people wonder how long it will be before I prophesy to the waiter or waitress. You've read about God moving in all kinds of different ways and in diverse places. This is because He is omnipresent; He is everywhere in each of our lives 24 hours a day When I go a grocery or department store it's not uncommon for me to stop and prophesy to someone in the store. There are even occasions when God directs me to stop and ask somebody if I can pray for their healing.

I believe that God wants to work through all of us that He might manifest His love and His power on the face of this planet. He is looking for ordinary people to do it. You don't need a degree in theology. The first disciples of Jesus were ordinary men, most of them fisherman, one a tax collector, and the others we're really not told.

What was the key to their power? I believe it was their relationship with Him. Acts 4:13 (NKJV) says, *"Now when they saw the boldness of Peter and John, and perceived that they were uneducated and untrained men, they marveled. And they realized that they had been with Jesus."*

The voice of God is still saying, "Whom shall I send, And who will go for us?" We need to respond as Isaiah did, *"Then I said, 'Here am I! Send me.'"* Isaiah 6:8 (NKJV). Go ahead raise your hands and shout, "Here I am, send me!"

I want to encourage you to live in the spirit man because we were all called to abide there. I hope and pray that this book has been a source of encouragement to you. Like Jacob we need to be aware of God <u>always</u> being present. We read in Genesis 28:16 (NKJV), *"Then Jacob awoke from his sleep and said, 'Surely the Lord is in this place, and I did not know it.'"*

Lord, help us to always be aware of Your presence.

I pray that you will realize that you don't need to be in church or on a mission's trip for God to use you. May you truly see that God still uses ordinary people, and moreover, that He wants to use <u>you</u>!

I want to leave you with what I wrote on the back cover. Recently I came across the following verses in Daniel 4:1-3. These verses capture the heart of why I wanted to write <u>Divine Encounters.</u>

Like Nebuchadnezzar, I wanted to give a first-hand account of all the staggering miracles and wonders I have seen in while walking with the Lord for 48 years. Here is what Daniel wrote. *"King Nebuchadnezzar to everyone, everywhere—every race, color, and creed: 'Peace and prosperity to all! It is my privilege to report to you the gracious miracles that the High God has done for me.' His miracles are staggering, his wonders are surprising. His kingdom lasts and lasts, his sovereign rule goes on forever."* The Message Bible

I so desire that each person who reads this book would be persuaded to have their own "Divine Encounter" with the living God, that they would be drawn into a deeper relationship with Him, and finally, like the Apostle Paul, would cry out saying, *"All I want is to know Christ and the power that raised him to life."* Philippians 3:10 (CEV)

Perhaps the old song we heard as a child will once again capture our hearts. "Jesus loves me, yes I know, because the Bible tells me so." I pray that you would discover how much you are loved by Abba, that you and I were not created to perform, but to be His sons and daughters .

When I see pictures that portray Jesus on the cross and his arms outstretched, I can hear him say, "This is how much I love you."

Thank you for reading this book. I pray that it has and will be a source of encouragement for you.

Please know this: WE ARE ALL SPECIAL IN OUR FATHER'S EYES.

I pray God's very best for your life!

PB

About the Author

Pastor Brian R. Weeks began ministering in 1972 and has served as a pastor to both youths and young adults. He has also served as an associate pastor, and then for 25 years as a senior pastor, apostolic missionary, and church planter. In March of 2017 he released his church Solomon's Porch but continues to serve among its several pastors in order to remain part of the local church.

In 2008 Pastor Brian formed *Brian Weeks Ministries* to facilitate his call to travel nationally and internationally. His travels have taken him to Haiti, Ukraine, India, and Romania, and into Evangelical, Charismatic, Episcopal, Catholic, Black Pentecostal, Dutch Reform, Vineyard, Methodist, Baptist, and Faith churches.

His ministry includes teaching and training leaders and pastors through pastors' and youth conferences and Bible schools as well as doing prophetic ministry in these same settings.

Pastor Brian has co-planted two churches and has planted three others. His most recent church plant was birthed on Christmas Eve 2009. With his rich and diversified experience, he loves encouraging and mentoring other pastors in the Holy Spirit, as well as helping them grow and develop their churches into their futures.

Pastor Brian's passion is to see lives transformed by the power and love of God. His strong desire is that God's sons and daughters would not only discover their gifts and talents, but more importantly comprehend how much God delights in them and how affectionately they are loved, knowing full well that they were created for a divine purpose. Pastor Brian's prophetic ministry helps people grasp these realities and empowers them to take steps towards their tomorrows. One of his greatest joys is to see people enjoy the presence of God and cherish their relationship with the Lord and His people.

Pastor Brian lives in Rehoboth, Massachusetts with his wife Donna of forty-five years. They have two adult children.

CPSIA information can be obtained
at www.ICGtesting.com
Printed in the USA
BVOW06s1127270817
493033BV00009B/15/P